SCHOLASTIC Guide to

Gra

M

as

Scholastic Inc.

New York Toronto London Auckland

Sydney Mexico City New Delhi Hong Kong

To my granddaughter, Summer Valentine—
the best grammar I know is this subject,
verb, and direct object: "I love you."

ISBN 978-0-545-35669-5

10 9 8 7 6 5 4 3 2 1   11 12 13 14 15

Printed in the U.S.A.   40
First printing, September 2010
Revised edition, August 2011
Book design by Kay Petronio
Illustrations by Elliot Cowan

Contents

INTRODUCTION

Meet Marvin Terban, featured in this book as **Professor Grammar!**

Have you ever wondered how many languages there are in the world? Nobody knows for sure, but some word experts think there could be as many as 6,000, from Ani, a language of Botswana, to Zyphe, which is spoken in Myanmar (Burma).

English is one of the most popular languages in the world. Almost a billion people use English as their first or second language. That's lucky for me, because that's the language I know the best. That gives me a lot of people to talk to; send letters, e-mails, text messages, or tweets to; or just say Hi! to on the street.

Wherever you go in the world, you will speak, hear, read, and write English. It's hard to get lost on the subways of Tokyo, Japan, because the signs are in English and Japanese. You can buy an English-language newspaper in every major city of the world. When a plane from Asia lands in South America, the pilot and the air traffic controller speak to each other in English. Scientists, politicians, educators, and businesspeople from many different countries speak to one another exclusively in English. The number of people who are learning English in China today is about the same as the number of people who live in the whole United States!

So it's very important for us to use the best English we can every day. When you write a paper in school, meet new people, apply to college, or try to get a job, you will want to get your ideas across in the best possible way—with no embarrassing mistakes.

But English is very tricky. There are more words in English than in most other major languages. Spelling can be a real challenge. You have to capitalize the right words. Correct punctuation sometimes baffles even college professors.

Don't worry. I will help you. Just look in the index that begins on page 253 to find any topic you need. Soon you'll have about a billion people— including me!—to say Hi! to in excellent English.

The Parts of Speech

To build a house, you need building materials, like wood, metal, and glass. To build a language, you need building materials, too. They're called the **Parts of Speech**, and there are eight of them:

verbs

nouns

adjectives

adverbs

prepositions

pronouns

conjunctions

interjections

There are over 600,000 words in the English language, and every word fits into at least one of these eight categories.

VERBS

A verb is a word that shows action.

  Verbs can show vigorous action like running, jumping, and bouncing, or quiet action like thinking, dreaming, and looking.

The verb to be shows just being, not doing: am, are, is, was, were, be, being, been.

Tenses

Tense means the time at which the action, being, or doing happens. There are six main tenses.

The **present** tense expresses an action that is happening right now.

> She *sees* the tap-dancing octopus.

The **past** tense expresses an action that has already happened.

> She *saw* the baby flying in the hot-air balloon.

The **future** tense expresses an action that is going to happen.

> She *will see* amazing sights on her trip to Mars.

The **present perfect** tense expresses an action that was started in the past and has just finished or is still continuing.

She *has seen* what she wanted to see, and now she's going home.

The **past perfect** tense expresses an action in the past that was completed before another action in the past.

She *had seen* everything in the museum before it closed.

The **future perfect** tense expresses an action that will be begun and completed in the future.

She *will have seen* the "Happy Birthday" sign before we shout "Happy Birthday!" and the surprise will be ruined.

Helping Verbs

There are twenty-three common helping verbs (sometimes called auxiliary verbs). They're not too hard to remember if you think of them like this:

3 Ds: do, does, did
3 Hs: have, has, had
3 Ms: may, must, might
3 Bs: be, being, been
2 Ws: was, were
3 -ould's: should, could, would
2 -ll's: shall, will
The present tense of the verb to be: am, are, is
Now put them all into a can.

A full verb phrase can have one, two, three, or four different verbs: one main verb and up to three helping verbs.

> You go.

> You have gone.

> You will have gone.

> You should have been going.

Regular and Irregular Verbs

Most verbs in English are regular. To form the past tense of these, you just add -d or -ed.

> Today it walks. Last week it walked. It has always walked.

> Today it dances. Last week it danced. It has always danced.

For irregular verbs, on the other hand, the past tense is formed in different ways. That's why they're called "irregular." Here are some examples.

Today I . . . (Present)	Yesterday I . . . (Past)	I have . . . (Past Participle)
begin	began	begun
drink	drank	drunk
fly	flew	flown
shake	shook	shaken
speak	spoke	spoken
take	took	taken
wear	wore	worn

NOUNS

A **noun** is a word that names a person, place, thing, or idea.

There are more nouns in English than any other kind of word, because there are so many people, places, things, and ideas in the world to name.

In the short paragraph below, there are twenty nouns.

Consuela, a **girl** in my **class**, lived in the **country** of **Brookliana** until she was three **years** old. Then she and her **family** traveled with great **courage** by **horse**, **bus**, **boat**, and **plane**, over **mountains**, **jungles**, and **oceans**, to get to **Boston**. Their **house** is on **Renae Road**, near the **mall** that sells those tap-dancing **piglets**.

Articles

The, **a**, and **an** are called *articles*. They are also called *noun signals*, because they signal you that a noun is coming up in the sentence. The noun could be the next word, or it could come a few words later, but if you see **the**, **a**, or **an** in a sentence, you can be sure you're going to find a noun soon.

The dog buried **a** bone.
    noun   *noun*

The huge, brown, furry dog buried **a** huge, brown, furry bone.
                 noun   *noun*

Kinds of Nouns

A noun can be—

Common—the name of any person, place, thing, or idea:

boy, city, toothpick, liberty

Proper—the name of a specific person, place, or thing:

Peter, Chicago, Rocky Mountains

When a noun is proper, it's always capitalized. See *Capitalization* on pages 82—87.

 Sometimes two or more words together make one proper noun: Empire State Building, Okefenokee Swamp, Sea of Japan, Lake Titicaca, Central Park West.

Concrete—a person, place, or thing that you can perceive with any of your five senses—sight, hearing, smell, touch, or taste:

gorilla, pizza, tulip, raindrops, mud, computer, valentine

Abstract—a feeling, emotion, passion, idea, or quality:

sadness, freedom, honesty, intelligence, patience

Even though you can't see, taste, hear, smell, or touch feelings and emotions, they really do exist, and the words that name them are called *abstract nouns*.

Some abstract nouns can be proper, especially in poetry, poetic writing, or words to songs:

The passions that burn in you and me
Are Love and Life and Liberty!

Collective—a group of persons, places, or things:

staff, faculty, bouquet, audience, team, flock,

assembly, bundle, nation

Even though collective nouns include many people, animals, or things, they are still singular nouns, not plural, because everyone or everything in the group is acting together as one.

The orchestra *is* (not *are*) performing at eight o'clock.

Compound—two or more words used together as one noun:

earthquake, jellyfish, football

rush hour, fairy tale

battle-ax, sister-in-law, drive-in

Did you notice that compound nouns can be written as one word, two separate words, or two words connected with a hyphen? Most compound nouns are single words without hyphens, but if you're not sure, check your dictionary or spell-checker. See <u>Hyphens</u> on page 116.

Uses of Nouns

A noun is the busiest part of speech. Nouns can be used in the following nine ways.

SUBJECT

The subject is the word that names the person, place, thing, or idea that a sentence is about. Every sentence must have a subject. Without a subject, there's no sentence. The subject always performs the action of the verb.

To find the subject, first find the verb and ask yourself, "Who or what is doing this?" The answer will be the subject.

An elephant the size of Toledo nimbly walked across the tightrope while juggling three watermelons.

What's the verb? *Walked*. Who walked? *An elephant*. So *elephant* is the subject of the sentence. The sentence is about the elephant.

COMPLETE SUBJECTS AND SIMPLE SUBJECTS

In the sentence about the elephant, *elephant* is the subject. Since it's only one word, we call it the *simple subject*. The six words *an elephant the size of Toledo* are called the *complete subject*. The complete subject is the simple subject and all its modifiers (the adjectives, adverbs, prepositional phrases, etc., that go with it). See pages 21, 23, and 25 to learn more.

A simple subject can sometimes be more than one word when the words go together to name one person, place, or thing.

The Golden Gate Bridge in San Francisco Bay was opened in 1937 and for over twenty-five years was the longest suspension bridge in the world.

In the sentence above, *The Golden Gate Bridge* is the simple subject, because all those words name just one bridge. *The Golden Gate Bridge in San Francisco Bay* is the complete subject.

Sometimes the simple subject is also the complete subject.

Rachel tripped over her shoelace and fell right into the barrel of spaghetti sauce.

Rachel is the simple subject and the complete subject all in one word.

DIRECT OBJECT

The *direct object* is the noun that receives the action of the verb. While every sentence has to have a subject, not every sentence has a direct object, but many sentences do.

To find the direct object, first find the verb. Then ask yourself, "Who or what is the action being done to? Who or what is receiving the action of the verb?" That's the direct object.

The captain of the football team kicked the coconut over the palm trees.

What's the verb? *Kicked.* Who or what got kicked? *The coconut.* So *coconut* is the direct object. It didn't do anything. Something was done to it.

OBJECT OF A PREPOSITION

A *prepositional phrase* is a group of words that starts with a preposition and ends with a noun (or pronoun) called the *object of the preposition*. The object of the preposition completes the meaning of the preposition. If you write, "She threw the ball to . . ." and leave the sentence like that, it isn't complete. If you write, "She threw the ball to her dog," the word *dog* completes the meaning of the preposition *to*. *Dog* is the object of the preposition *to*.

In the following sentences, the prepositional phrases are in italics (letters that slant to the right) and the objects of the prepositions are in boldface.

While I was snorkeling, I saw fantastic fish *under the* **water**.

Inside his **pockets** were treasures too amazing to believe.

See *Prepositions* on page 24.

PREDICATE NOUN

The *predicate noun* always comes after the verb *to be* and always means the same thing as the subject of the sentence.

Mad Murgatroy is the king of this country and can have you dipped in chocolate if he wants to!

What's the verb? *Is*. Who is? *Mad Murgatroy*. That's the subject. What is he? *King*. *King* is the predicate noun. Mad Murgatroy and king are the same person. Mad Murgatroy is the king and the king is Mad Murgatroy.

Sometimes a predicate noun is called a **predicate nominative**.

NOUN OF DIRECT ADDRESS

When you are speaking or writing directly to a person, you sometimes call him or her by name or title. The noun that indicates that name or title is the *noun of direct address*. The noun of direct address can be a common noun or a proper noun.

I must ask you, *Mrs. Schlepkis*, to stop chewing on the leaves of my Venus flytrap plant.

Kid, will you please help me carry this grand piano up to the twelfth floor?

Who is being spoken to in these sentences? *Mrs. Schlepkis* and *kid*. Those nouns are the nouns of direct address, because they name the people who are being addressed (spoken to) directly.

See *Punctuating Nouns of Direct Address* on page 110.

INDIRECT OBJECT OF THE VERB

The *indirect object* names the person, place, thing, or idea that receives the action of the verb indirectly.

The monkey sold the rhino his favorite banana.

What's the verb? *Sold*. To whom was the banana sold? *The rhino*. That's the indirect object, because it's receiving the action of the verb *sold* indirectly. (*Banana* is the direct object, because that's what was sold.)

The monkey baked the rhino a banana cream pie.

What's the verb? *Baked*. What was baked? *A banana cream pie*. That's the direct object. For whom was it baked? *The rhino*. That's the indirect object.

The indirect object always comes before the direct object.

Here's a tip for finding the indirect object. You can sometimes imagine that the word *to* or the word *for* is in front of the indirect object even though *to* and *for* aren't there.

to

The monkey sold ^ the rhino his favorite banana.

for

The monkey baked ^ the rhino a banana cream pie.

> Here are some verbs that regularly have indirect objects
> after them: <u>give</u>, <u>throw</u>, <u>send</u>, <u>show</u>, and <u>buy</u>.

APPOSITIVE

An appositive is a noun or a phrase that

    ı. comes after another noun, or

    2. gives information about that noun.

<u>**Herman**</u>, <u>**the world's tallest person**</u>, cleans the
 noun   *noun*

windows in his apartment without a ladder, and he lives on the
ninth floor!

The world's tallest person comes after *Herman* and gives information
about him. *Herman* and *the world's tallest person* are said to be "in
apposition" with each other.

    See *Punctuating Appositives* on page 110.

POSSESSIVE NOUN

Possession means *ownership*. A *possessive noun* names the person,
place, or thing that owns something or has a very close relationship with
someone.

George Washington's wooden teeth were on display at the exhibit.

George Washington's wife was named Martha.

All possessive nouns must have apostrophes. See *Apostrophes* on page 97—102.

OBJECT COMPLEMENT

Sometimes a direct object is not enough by itself and needs another word to finish the meaning of the sentence. An *object complement* is the word that completes the direct object.

Last year they elected my uncle *chief zookeeper*.

What's the verb? *Elected*. Who got elected? *My uncle*. That's the direct object. What did he get elected? *Chief zookeeper*. That's the object complement. Without those words, we wouldn't know what job my uncle was elected to.

The lady next door calls her pet skunk Perfume.

What's the direct object? *Pet skunk*. What is it called? *Perfume*. That's the object complement, because without it we wouldn't know what the neighbor calls her skunk. It completes the direct object.

A fun way to remember the nine uses of nouns is to remember **DIP A SPOON:**

> **D**irect Object
> **I**ndirect Object
> **P**redicate Noun
> **A**ppositive
> **S**ubject
> **P**ossessive Noun
> **O**bject of the Preposition
> **O**bject Complement
> **N**oun of Direct Address

ADJECTIVES

An adjective is a word that describes (or modifies) a noun or a pronoun.

Modify means to qualify or limit the meaning of something. If you say "lizard," you could mean any lizard in the world, but if you say "old, wrinkly lizard," you are limiting—or modifying—your meaning to just lizards that are old and wrinkly. You are not talking about any lizards that are young or smooth.

An adjective usually answers one of three questions about the noun it is describing:

What kind of? "a *yellow* cat" What kind of cat? *Yellow.*

How many? "*sixteen* jelly beans" How many jelly beans? *Sixteen.*

Which one or which ones? "*those* dinosaur bones" Which dinosaur bones? *Those.*

An adjective can come right in front of the noun it modifies:

America is a *free* country, and many *brave* people live here.

An adjective can come after a linking verb (like the verb *to be*):

America is *free*, and her people are *brave*.

An adjective can even stand alone without the noun it is describing:

America is the land of the *free* and the home of the *brave*.

In the example above, you can assume that the sentence means that America is the land of free people and brave people, even though the word *people* isn't in the sentence.

Common and Proper Adjectives

Just as nouns can be common and proper (see *Kinds of Nouns* on page 12), so can adjectives.

A **common** adjective is a regular adjective, like *happy*, *huge*, *sloppy*, or *wonderful*.

A **proper** adjective comes from a proper noun and is always capitalized.

Proper Nouns	Proper Adjectives
Japan	Japanese
Venice	Venetian
Florida	Floridian
Queen Victoria	Victorian
Finland	Finnish

France	French
Shakespeare	Shakespearean
Holland	Dutch

ADVERBS

An adverb is a word that describes or modifies a verb, an adjective, or another adverb.

> You can always remember what adverbs modify if you think of the name **AVA**: **A**dverbs, **V**erbs, **A**djectives.

Adverbs answer these questions:

Where? (The hen laid the egg *there*.)

When? (It happened *yesterday*.)

How? (She cackled *loudly* when the egg came out.)

To what extent? (She was *extremely* proud.)

An adverb modifying a verb:

He <u>played</u> the tuba <u>*loudly*</u>.
　　verb　　　　　　adverb

An adverb modifying an adverb:

He played the tuba <u>*unbelievably*</u> <u>loudly</u>.
　　　　　　　　adverb　　　adverb

An adverb modifying an adjective:

His tuba playing was <u>*amazingly*</u> <u>loud</u>.
　　　　　　　　adverb　　adjective

PREPOSITIONS

A *preposition* is a word that shows how one word in a sentence relates to another.

A preposition often shows location, direction, or time.

Location: My little brother is hiding *under* the dirty laundry. (Where is he located? *Under* the laundry.)

Direction: My little brother is falling *into* the bowl of raspberry syrup. (Where is he falling? *Into* the syrup.)

Time: *After* lunch, I have to give my little brother a bath. (When do I give him the bath? *After* lunch.)

Relationship between words: My little brother always wants to go *with* me wherever I go. (What is the relationship between my brother and me? He wants to go *with* me.)

There are thousands and thousands of nouns and verbs in English, but only about sixty prepositions.

Here are some of the most common.

about	at	down	of	to
above	before	during	off	toward
across	behind	for	on	under
after	below	from	out	until
against	beside	in	over	up
along	between	into	past	upon
among	beyond	like	round	with
around	by	near	through	without

Compound Prepositions

Sometimes two or more words together do the job of one preposition.
They are called *compound prepositions*. Here are some examples:

according to	because of	in addition to
ahead of	due to	in back of
away from	except for	instead of

He went to Jupiter *by way of* Neptune.

Romeo waited *in front of* Juliet's balcony.

Everyone failed *with the exception of* those who passed.

Prepositional Phrases

Every preposition begins a *prepositional phrase*. (*Phrase* means a group
of words.) The first word in a prepositional phrase is the preposition. The
last word is called the *object of the preposition*.

The shortest prepositional phrase possible is two words long.

The hamster ran **into it**.
  prep. obj. of prep

But prepositional phrases can be much longer.

The hamster ran **into** its **magnificent, soundproof,**
  prep.   obj. of prep.

air-conditioned, state-of-the-art, fully automated cage.
  obj. of prep.

PREPOSITION OR ADVERB?

Sometimes a word can be a preposition in one sentence and an adverb in the next. How can you tell? Easy. If there's a noun that's the object of the preposition after the word, it's a preposition. If there's no object, it's an adverb.

She ran out. (There's no object, so *out* is an adverb that's modifying the verb *ran* and answering the question "where?")

She ran out the door. (*Door* is the object of the preposition *out*, so *out* is a preposition here.)

PRONOUNS

A *pronoun* is a word that takes the place of a noun. A pronoun can be used almost every way a noun can be used. See *Uses of Nouns* on page 14.

If you didn't have pronouns, you would have to keep repeating the noun all the time, like this:

When Jennifer woke up that day, Jennifer realized that that day was Jennifer's birthday. "Jennifer is a teenager at last!" Jennifer cried. "Jennifer has waited thirteen long years to be a teenager. Jennifer deserves something special today, a birthday gift." Jennifer looked into Jennifer's mirror and saw Jennifer. "Jennifer wonders what Jennifer will give Jennifer on Jennifer's special day," Jennifer said to Jennifer in the mirror.

It sounds much better, and definitely not as weird, when you replace some of the nouns with pronouns.

When Jennifer woke up that day, **she** realized that **it** was **her** birthday. "**I** am a teenager at last!" **she** cried. "**I** have waited thirteen long years to be a teenager. **I** deserve something special today, a birthday gift." **She** looked into **her** mirror and saw **herself**. "**I** wonder what **I** will give you on **your** special day," **she** said to **herself** in the mirror.

These *personal pronouns* are divided into three groups: *subject pronouns*, *object pronouns*, and *possessive pronouns*.

Subject Pronouns (used for subjects)

I, you, he, she, it, we, they

Object Pronouns (used for direct objects, indirect objects, and objects of prepositions)

me, you, him, her, it, us, them

Possessive Pronouns (used to show ownership)

my, mine, your, yours, his, her, hers, its, our, ours, their, theirs

Besides the personal pronouns listed above, there are many other pronouns that can take the place of nouns in sentences. Here are some examples:

anybody	nobody	what
both	nothing	which
each	several	who
everybody	some	whom
itself	something	whose
many	that	
neither	themselves	

CONJUNCTIONS

A **conjunction** is a word that joins together words or parts of a sentence.

Joining words together:

I'd like five peanut butter *and* jelly sandwiches, please.

Joining parts of a sentence together:

I ran as fast as I could, *but* the ice cream still melted.

There are dozens of conjunctions. Here are some that you use every day:

although	because	if
since	though	unless
when	where	however
therefore	whenever	while

Sometimes conjunctions are used in pairs. They're called *correlative conjunctions*.

either/or	neither/nor	not only/but also
both/and	whether/or	just as/so

The three most-used conjunctions are <u>and</u>, <u>or</u>, and <u>but</u>.

INTERJECTIONS

An **interjection** is a word that shows strong feelings or emotions.

It is usually a short word that comes at the beginning of a sentence.

Here are some examples:

gadzooks	gosh	hey
hooray	oops	ouch
ugh	well	wow

An interjection can be followed by a comma or an exclamation point. If the interjection shows a really strong emotion, use an exclamation point. See Exclamation Points on page 116.

Oh, that baby chipmunk is adorable.

Oh! You've ruined my favorite pickle costume.

How the Parts of Speech Change

Sometimes a word's part of speech changes from one sentence to another. It all depends on how it's used.

adj.
The <u>down</u> escalator is not running, so we have to walk.

(**Down** is describing the escalator.)

noun
I sleep best when the pillow is filled with <u>down</u>.

(**Down** means feathers. Feathers are things.)

adv.

The apatosaurus fell <u>down</u> and made the building rumble.

(**Down** modifies the verb *fell* and answers the question "Where did the brontosaurus fall?")

verb

Did the dragon <u>down</u> the knight with just one swipe of her tail?

(**Down** is a word that shows action: knocking someone to the ground.)

prep.

The sprightly squirrel ran <u>down</u> the tree.

(**Down** is the first word in the prepositional phrase "down the tree." It shows direction.)

Sentences and Paragraphs

SENTENCES

What is a sentence?

A sentence:

- is a group of words
- begins with a capital letter
- contains a complete subject and a complete predicate
- ends with one of three punctuation marks (**.** **?** or **!**)
- makes complete sense

Four Kinds of Sentences

There are four kinds of sentences, demonstrated in the little dialogue below: **declarative**, **interrogative**, **exclamatory**, and **imperative**. Every sentence in every book, newspaper, magazine, story, blog, text message, and e-mail that you have ever read fits into one of these four categories.

"You have a banana in your ear."

"What did you say?"

"You have a banana in your ear!"

"Please speak more loudly. I have a banana in my ear."

Declarative Sentence

"You have a banana in your ear."

This kind of sentence declares a fact, makes a statement, or gives information. It always ends with a period.

Interrogative Sentence

"What did you say?"

This kind of sentence asks a question. (To *interrogate* means to question.) It always ends with a question mark.

Exclamatory Sentence

"You have a banana in your ear!"

This kind of sentence exclaims or cries out with strong emotions or feelings (like anger, frustration, happiness, disgust, surprise, shock, or horror). It always ends with an exclamation point (also called an exclamation mark).

Imperative Sentence

"Please speak more loudly."

This kind of sentence makes a request, asks a favor, or gives a command. It ends with a period if it expresses a polite request or gives a mild order, like "Please be seated." If it expresses strong emotions, it ends with an exclamation point, like this: "Give me back my chocolate-covered grasshopper this instant!"

You (Understood)

Every imperative sentence has a subject, even though it's not always expressed in the sentence. The subject of every imperative sentence is you. Because the reader or listener sometimes has to understand that you is the subject, it's called you (understood). "Sit down" really means "You, sit down."

Some sentences sound like questions, but they're really imperative sentences that are making requests or giving orders. They end with periods, not question marks.

"Will you kindly take that lamp shade off your head."

"Can you answer my question without whistling."

Imagine four friends talking, and try to identify the four kinds of sentences in the dialogue on the next page.

"There's a test today." (That's a statement of fact.)

"What's on it?" (Obviously a question.)

"I forgot to study!" (Somebody's panicking.)

"Lend me your notes." (This person needs a favor.)

If you said *declarative*, *interrogative*, *exclamatory*, and *imperative*, in that order, you are right!

Subjects and Predicates

THE TWO MAIN PARTS OF EVERY SENTENCE

Every sentence can be divided into two parts: the *complete subject* and the *complete predicate*. Everything in a sentence that is not the complete subject is the complete predicate. Everything in a sentence that is not the complete predicate is the complete subject.

What is the complete subject? The subject is the person, place, thing, or idea that the sentence is about. It performs the action of the verb. The complete subject is usually a noun or pronoun and all the words that go with it.

How do you find the complete subject? First find the verb (the word that shows action or being). Then ask yourself "Who or what is doing this? Who or what is the sentence about?" The answer will be the complete subject. Everything else in the sentence will be the complete predicate.

See *Verbs* on page 8 and *Subject* on page 14.

Complete Subject

Mrs. Freedman from Ledgewood Way

Complete Predicate

has two children, four grandchildren, and one husband.

Both a complete subject and a complete predicate can be many words long or just one word.

Complete Subject

The Universal Museum of Old-Fashioned Inventions on the corner of Shurtleff and Shawmut Streets

Complete Predicate

closed.

Complete Subject

She

Complete Predicate

put a bowl of cherries, bananas, and strawberries on her head and started dancing the fandango to everyone's delight.

VERB

The verb is always in the complete predicate. Some people call the verb the simple predicate.

The **simple subject** is usually one or two main words inside the complete subject, without all the adjectives, adverbs, phrases, and other words that go with it. In the sentence below, the complete subject is nine words long, but the simple subject is only one word long.

Complete Subject

The tall, bearded history teacher on the third floor

Simple Subject

teacher

Sometimes the complete subject is just one word, so it is also the simple subject.

Roslyn used to work for the telephone company before she retired to raise puppies.

A complete sentence can be as short as two words.

She laughed.

She is the complete subject. *Laughed* is the complete predicate.

A complete sentence can be as short as one word if that one word is an imperative verb. "Stop!" is a complete imperative sentence. Stop is the complete predicate, and you (understood) is the complete subject, even though it's not expressed.

See *Imperative Sentence* on page 32.
See *You (Understood)* on page 33.

Word Order

In most sentences, the complete subject comes before the complete predicate.

> Three wild men in gorilla costumes charged out of the mouth of the dark cave.

But sometimes, for variety, the predicate can come first.

> Out of the mouth of the dark cave charged three wild men in gorilla costumes.

Sometimes the complete subject can come in the middle of the complete predicate. In the sentence below, the complete subject is in boldface. Part of the complete predicate is before it, and part is after it.

> In the early days of our history, **Benjamin Franklin** wanted the national bird of the United States to be a turkey, not an eagle.

Compound Subjects and Compound Predicates

Sometimes a verb can have more than one subject.

> Jessica and Aaron took Jade for a walk.

Jessica and *Aaron* are compound subjects. (*Compound* means two working together.)

Sometimes a subject can have more than one verb.

> Jade laughed and played the whole day.

Laughed and *played* are called compound verbs.

Fragments and How to Fix Them

Sometimes a group of words begins with a capital letter, ends with a period, question mark, or exclamation mark, and looks like a sentence but doesn't express a complete thought. Usually the subject or the predicate is missing. A group of words like this is called a *fragment* (a part of a sentence, but not the whole thing). A fragment can be short or long.

> Strapping on his trusty parachute and jumping out the door of the high-flying plane into the frigid night air.
> (There's no subject.)

> The old man with the long gray beard and the multicolored freckles on his bulbous nose.
> (There's no predicate.)

Fixing Fragments

Since a fragment has missing parts, you have to fill in what's missing to fix it.

Fragment (with a missing subject):

Whooping and hollering after winning the championship.

Fixed sentence:

My high school football team was whooping and hollering after winning the championship.

Fragment (with a missing predicate):

A baboon with multicolored feathers in its hair and large earrings shaped like pineapples.

Fixed sentence:

A baboon with multicolored feathers in its hair and large earrings shaped like pineapples was handing out free honey-roasted peanuts as people came into the circus.

Remember, a sentence has a subject and a predicate, and it makes complete sense.

Clauses

A clause is a group of words that contains a subject and a verb. If the clause makes complete sense and can stand alone and be a sentence by itself, it's called a main clause.

The moon rose at 7:18 tonight.

Other names for main clause are principal clause and independent clause. People use all three names for a clause that can be a sentence by itself.

If the clause cannot stand alone and express a complete thought, it's called a dependent clause. (It depends on another clause to make a whole sentence.)

As I was looking out the car window, the moon rose at 7:18 tonight.

As I was looking out the car window does not express a complete thought and could not be a sentence by itself. Therefore, it is a dependent clause.

Another name for a dependent clause is a subordinate clause. People use the two names interchangeably.

Simple, Compound, and Complex Sentences

Simple Sentence

If a sentence is made up of one main (principal, independent) clause, it's called a simple sentence.

He ran out into the street in his underwear.

Compound Sentence

If you put two or more main clauses together, you have a compound sentence.

He was frightened by the strange noises coming from his closet, and he ran out into the street in his underwear.

That sentence is made up of two clauses that could each be a separate sentence. The clauses are related in meaning, and one is just as important as the other. They are connected by a comma plus the conjunction *and*.

Complex Sentence

If you combine an independent (main, principal) clause with a dependent (subordinate) clause, you have a complex sentence. It doesn't matter which clause comes first.

When he heard strange noises coming from his closet, he ran out into the street in his underwear.

He ran out into the street in his underwear when he heard strange noises coming from his closet.

Run-On Sentences and How to Fix Them

If main clauses are connected by a comma, that's a run-on sentence, and that's not good. A comma is too weak to hold main clauses together.

> The rocket ship landed on Jupiter, the astronauts shouted, "Hooray!"

A run-on sentence can be fixed in several ways:

1. Add a conjunction after the comma:

> The rocket ship landed on Jupiter, and the astronauts shouted, "Hooray!"

2. Connect the clauses with a semicolon:

> The rocket ship landed on Jupiter; the astronauts shouted, "Hooray!"

> See *Conjunctions* on page 28 and *Semicolons* on page 123.

3. Change one of the independent clauses to a dependent clause:

> When the rocket ship landed on Jupiter, the astronauts shouted, "Hooray!"

4. Start a new sentence:

> The rocket ship landed on Jupiter. The astronauts shouted, "Hooray!"

Try to avoid having too many short sentences in a row. Use a combination of short sentences and longer compound and complex sentences to make your writing more varied and interesting.

PARAGRAPHS

What Is a Paragraph?

Just as words go together to make sentences, sentences go together to make paragraphs. A paragraph is a group of sentences that all relate to the same thought or topic. The sentences move the main idea along.

Most paragraphs are about two to six sentences long. A paragraph with a lot of details can be longer.

A one-sentence paragraph can be dramatic or unexpected, especially if it comes after several longer paragraphs.

And that was the last she ever heard from her brother's gerbil!

How to Write a Good Paragraph

When you write a paragraph in an essay or in a report, start with a topic sentence that states the main idea and tells what the paragraph is about in a general way. The sentences that follow should support that topic and add new facts, information, details, or examples. The last sentence usually sums up the main idea of the paragraph or restates it in different words.

Topic sentence: states the main idea

Supporting sentences: give details, examples, etc.

Last sentence: sums up or restates the main idea

When to Start a New Paragraph

Start a new paragraph when you write about a new idea or a different aspect of the same idea. Start a new paragraph when the time, action, place, speaker, or characters change. You should also start a new paragraph if the one you're writing is starting to get too long.

My Birthday

My birthday this year was great! It was on a Saturday, so I could sleep late. My dad made my favorite breakfast: crispy waffles with fruit on top. After breakfast, I helped my mom put together my new bike, and then I went to the ball game. I pitched for five innings and struck out the other team's three best players.

That night, we all went to Sloppy Pete's Pizza Palace, and I ordered a super-special with pepperoni and sausage. It came with a birthday candle in it. Then I got to choose a movie with my friends. We saw *Dinosaur Monsters Eat the World*! My little brother kept his eyes shut through most of it. I hope all my birthdays are as great as this one.

Make sure that all the sentences work together to explain the same basic idea. If any sentence doesn't belong, cut it out. For example, the following sentence would not belong in the story "My Birthday":

Last year, on my aunt's birthday, we had Indian food.

Even though it's about eating at a restaurant on someone's birthday, it's not about the writer's birthday.

The topic sentence is usually the first sentence, but sometimes, for variety, it could be at the end, like this:

At Cute Creatures, the giant cockatoo almost bit my nose. The turtle dove into its tank and splashed my new jacket. I almost stepped on the rabbit that was loose, the snake hissed at me, and a tiny puppy barked loudly in my ear when I nuzzled it. A trip to a pet store can sometimes be hazardous to your health.

CHAPTER THREE

Spelling: Getting the Letters Right

WHY IS SPELLING SO IMPORTANT?

There are hundreds of thousands of words in English, and several common misspellings. So you have a lot of chances to spell a word wrong.

Correct spelling is important to you because when you write a book report, a letter, a text message, an article for the school newspaper, a story, or even a note to your parents that you stick onto the refrigerator, you want your readers to understand you. Misspelled words can confuse your readers.

Besides, you don't want to be embarrassed by misspelled words. Too many wrong words in your writing can be mortifying.

What about Spell-Checkers?

It's really important to learn the main spelling rules, even if you have a spell-checker on your computer. (Besides, you don't always write on a computer.)

Want proof? Below is a little letter from a mother whose son is in trouble at school. If you read the letter aloud, it will sound perfect. But if you look at it closely, you'll see that it contains thirty-seven spelling mistakes! And the spell-checker missed every one of them. Find out why after you read the letter.

> Deer Principle,
> Eye due knot want two waist you're thyme. Aye herd my buoy did something that was knot aloud.
> Aisle bee inn too sea ewe at fore, sew pleas weight four me. Heal bee write their two, even if it reigns. Wee no yule bee fare with hymn when we meat yew.
> Buy.

Now here's the same letter with all the mistakes corrected.

> Dear Principal,
> I do not want to waste your time. I heard my boy did something that was not allowed.
> I'll be in to see you at four, so please wait for me. He'll be right there too, even if it rains. We know you'll be fair with him when we meet you.
> Bye.

Why did the spell-checker miss every mistake? Because the mistakes aren't spelling mistakes. These words are *homonyms* (sometimes called *homophones*), words that sound the same as other words but have different spellings and meanings. Your spell-checker can't check for homonyms, because there's nothing wrong with their spelling.

> ### Vowels and Consonants
> Before we get to the spelling rules, let's just make sure we get vowels and consonants straight. Remember that *a, e, i, o, u,* and sometimes *y* are the vowels. All the other letters are the consonants.

Seventeen Super Spelling Rules

Read on to learn what to do when you're stuck in one of these seventeen sticky spelling situations!

1. Divide longer words into parts.
2. The silent e. Drop it? Keep it?
3. Double the final consonant.
4. Change y to i.
5. ie or ei?
6. When two vowels go walking . . .
7. Plurals of nouns
8. Adding prefixes
9. Adding suffixes
10. Silent letters
11. -able or -ible?
12. Add k to verbs ending with c.

1. Divide longer words into parts.

You'll sometimes have better luck spelling a long word correctly if you try to sound it out part by part and then learn each part separately.

For instance, *superintendent*. Think of it as *super in ten dent*. Four short sounds are always easier to spell than one long one.

This plan won't work as well if the word has a totally weird spelling, especially at the beginning. But try it. It works pretty well if there are little words inside the bigger word. It will probably work with words like:

abundance	(a bun dance)
amendment	(a mend ment)
attendance	(at tend dance)
bungalow	(bung a low)
countenance	(count en ance)
dormitory	(dorm i tor y)
enlargement	(en large ment)
extraordinary	(ex tra or din ary)
fundamental	(fun da men tal)
government	(gov ern ment)
handkerchief	(hand ker chief)

ignoramus	(ig nor a mus)
kindergarten	(kin der gar ten)
ligament	(lig a ment)
maintenance	(main ten ance)
nevertheless	(never the less)
opportunity	(op por tun i ty)
propaganda	(prop a gan da)
refrigerator	(re frig er a tor)
significant	(sig ni fi cant)
thermometer	(ther mom e ter)
uniform	(un i form)

See *Watch out for those first few letters* on page 76.

2. The silent e. Drop it? Keep it?

If an e isn't pronounced at the end of a word, drop it when you add a suffix that begins with a vowel (like -ed, -ing, -age, -able, -ance, -al, -ible, -or, and -ous).

adventure	+ ous	= adventurous
arrive	+ al	= arrival
dance	+ ed	= danced
decorate	+ or	= decorator
force	+ ible	= forcible
guide	+ ance	= guidance
love	+ able	= lovable
store	+ age	= storage

The "drop the silent e" rule is used most often when you add -ing to a verb.

write	+ ing	= writing
come	+ ing	= coming
dine	+ ing	= dining
hope	+ ing	= hoping
scare	+ ing	= scaring
argue	+ ing	= arguing
become	+ ing	= becoming
give	+ ing	= giving
change	+ ing	= changing
encourage	+ ing	= encouraging
judge	+ ing	= judging
type	+ ing	= typing

Exceptions: As with many other rules, there are some exceptions to the "drop the silent e" rule.

Do not drop the silent e when the word ends with a soft -ge or a soft -ce and you're adding a suffix that begins with -ous or -able.

courage	+ ous	= courageous
outrage	+ ous	= outrageous
advantage	+ ous	= advantageous
change	+ able	= changeable
manage	+ able	= manageable
salvage	+ able	= salvageable
notice	+ able	= noticeable
pronounce	+ able	= pronounceable

| peace | + able | = peaceable |
| slice | + able | = sliceable |

For a few verbs that end with a silent e, we do not drop the e because if we did, they might be confused with other verbs.

For instance, the verb *singe* usually means to burn the ends of your hair by touching it briefly to a flame. If you dropped the silent e when you added -ing to *singe*, people would think the word was *singing*. That would make for a very bizarre sentence:

She was almost singing the ends of her eyelashes by leaning too close to the campfire.

So sing + ing = singing, and singe + ing = singeing. And a person could be singing a song and singeing her eyelashes all in one sentence!

In the same way, a dressmaker is *dyeing* a dress green, not *dying* it. (A plant that you forget to water is dying.) And a person who really, really wants to change the color of her dress could be dying to be dyeing it.

| singe | + ing | = singeing |
| dye | + ing | = dyeing |

Do not drop the silent e when you add -ing to four verbs that end with -oe.

hoe	+ ing	= hoeing
toe	+ ing	= toeing
canoe	+ ing	= canoeing
shoe	+ ing	= shoeing

Do not drop the silent e when you add -age to words that end in e.

| mile | + age | = mileage |
| acre | + age | = acreage |

Keep the silent e when you add a suffix that begins with a consonant: -teen, -ty, -less, -ly, -ment, -ful, etc.

nine	+ teen	= nineteen
nine	+ ty	= ninety
use	+ less	= useless
safe	+ ly	= safely
arrange	+ ment	= arrangement
care	+ ful	= careful
sure	+ ly	= surely
sincere	+ ly	= sincerely
immediate	+ ly	= immediately
definite	+ ly	= definitely
manage	+ ment	= management
use	+ ful	= useful

Exceptions: Of course, there are some exceptions to this rule too. (What would a rule be without exceptions?) Drop the silent e when adding a suffix that begins with a consonant in the following words.

nine	+ th	= ninth
true	+ ly	= truly
due	+ ly	= duly
argue	+ ment	= argument
acknowledge	+ ment	= acknowledgment

You can drop or keep the silent e in *judge* when you add -ment. Some dictionaries give both spellings. (Most dictionaries, however, give *judgment* as the preferred spelling.)

judge   + ment   = judgment *or* judgement

See *Words with different spellings* on page 74.

3. Double the final consonant

If a word ends with a single vowel and a single consonant, double the final consonant when you add a suffix that begins with a vowel (especially -ed, -er, and -ing).

Words that follow this rule end with letters like -an, -am, -ap, -ar, -el, -ep, -er, -et, -ip, -ol, -op, -ot, -ow, -ub, -ug, and -ur.

bar	+ ed	+ ing		= barred, barring
compel	+ ed	+ ing		= compelled, compelling
control	+ ed	+ ing		= controlled, controlling
forget		+ ing		= forgetting
occur	+ ed	+ ing		= occurred, occurring
plan	+ ed	+ ing	+ er	= planned, planning, planner
plot	+ ed	+ ing	+ er	= plotted, plotting, plotter
prefer	+ ed	+ ing		= preferred, preferring
slam	+ ed	+ ing		= slammed, slamming
slap	+ ed	+ ing		= slapped, slapping
scrub	+ ed	+ ing	+ er	= scrubbed, scrubbing, scrubber
step	+ ed	+ ing		= stepped, stepping
stop	+ ed	+ ing		= stopped, stopping

swim		+ ing	+ er	= swimming, swimmer
tip	+ ed	+ ing	+ er	= tipped, tipping, tipper
tug	+ ed	+ ing		= tugged, tugging
bag	+ age			= baggage
big	+ est			= biggest
control	+ able			= controllable
forbid	+ en			= forbidden
rebel	+ ion			= rebellion
remit	+ ance			= remittance

The words in the list above are all one-syllable words or longer words where the accent falls on the last syllable. Do not double the final consonant if the accent does not fall on the last syllable.

In the words below, the accent is not on the last syllable, so the final consonant is not doubled.

borrow	+ ed	+ ing	+ er	= borrowed, borrowing, borrower
develop	+ ed	+ ing	+ er	= developed, developing, developer
happen	+ ed	+ ing		= happened, happening
offer	+ ed	+ ing		= offered, offering
open	+ ed	+ ing	+ er	= opened, opening, opener
suffer	+ ed	+ ing	+ er	= suffered, suffering, sufferer
travel	+ ed	+ ing	+ er	= traveled, traveling, traveler

4. Change y to i.

When you add -es, -er, -est, or -ed to a word that ends with a consonant
and the letter *y*, change the *y* to *i*.

story	stories
family	families
enemy	enemies
lady	ladies
baby	babies
easy	easier, easiest
happy	happier, happiest
heavy	heavier, heaviest
lucky	luckier, luckiest
early	earlier, earliest
dirty	dirtier, dirtiest
busy	busier, busiest
hurry	hurries, hurried
study	studies, studied
try	tries, tried

5. ie or ei?

There's a famous poem that teachers and parents have been reciting for
years that's supposed to help kids decide whether a word is spelled with
ie or *ei*.

I before e
Except after c

Or when sounding like "a"
As in "neighbor" or "weigh."

The poem works for many words. Take the first line, for instance: *i before e*. All these words have *i* before *e*:

achieve	lie
believe	niece
brief	patient
chief	piece
field	priest
fiend	retrieve
friend	shield
pie	thief
grief	yield

The second line says: *except after c*. The following words have *e* before *i* because those letters come right after *c*:

ceiling	deceive
conceit	perceive
conceited	receipt
conceive	receive
deceit	

The last two lines of the poem are

Or when sounding like "a"
As in "neighbor" or "weigh."

The following words all have an *a* sound that is spelled *ei*:

beige	rein
deign	reindeer
eighty	skein
freight	sleigh
lei	veil
neigh	vein
neighbor	weigh
reign	weight

Exceptions

It would be great if the poem worked 100 percent of the time and always helped you to decide whether to spell a word with *ie* or *ei*. But there are exceptions to the poem.

There are words that have *i* before *e* even when they come after *c*.

ancient	scientist
deficient	society
efficient	species
financier	sufficient

There are words that have *e* before *i* and they don't come after *c*, and they don't sound like *a*.

caffeine	neither
codeine	protein
counterfeit	seismologist
either	seize

foreign	sheik
forfeit	sleight
heifer	sovereign
height	stein
kaleidoscope	their
leisure	weird

So what should you do with a spelling rule poem that has so many exceptions? You should learn the poem, but be familiar with the exceptions, too.

6. When two vowels go walking . . .

Your first- or second-grade teacher probably taught you the following rule, and it's still a good one: **When two vowels go walking, the first vowel does the talking.**

This rule doesn't work all the time, but it works with *ai*, *ea*, *oe*, and *oa* words. And there are a lot of those.

Think of *steamboat*. The letters *ea* in *steam* sound like the first letter, *e*. The letters *oa* in *boat* sound like the first letter, *o*. Many words follow this rule, including the following:

ai words		*ea* words		*oe* words	*oa* words
aid	mail	beam	peat	aloe	bloat
ail	main	beat	pearl	Crusoe	boast
aim	Maine	bleat	pleat	doe	boat
bail	nail	cheat	preach	floe	cloak
bait	paid	cleat	real	foe	coach
braid	pail	cream	ream	hoe	coal
brain	pain	crease	release	Joe	coast
chain	plain	deal	scream	Monroe	coat
claim	quail	defeat	seal	oboe	croak
drain	quaint	dream	seam	Poe	float
fail	raid	eager	seat	roe	foal
fair	rail	feat	shear	sloe	foam
flail	rain	flea	sneak	Tahoe	goal
frail	sail	gleam	speak	throe	goat
gain	stain	grease	squeak	toe	groan
gait	tail	heal	squeal	woe	Joan
grail	trail	heat	steal		load
grain	train	heave	steam		loam
jail	vail	leak	streak		loan
laid	vain	lease	stream		moan
lain	waif	meal	team		moat
lair	wail	mean	treat		poach
maid	wait	meat	veal		roach
	wraith	neat	weak		road
		peak	wheat		roam
		peal	wreath		roast
			zeal		shoal
					soak
					throat
					toad
					toast

7. Plurals of nouns

Singular means just one person, place, thing, or idea. *Plural* means two or more. For most nouns, you just add the letter *s* to make them plural.

Singular (just one)	Plural (more than one)
one smartphone	three smartphones
a basketball	a bag of basketballs
this shoe	this pair of shoes

If we could make all the nouns in English plural just by adding *s*, spelling plurals would be easy. But, of course, there are some nouns that are spelled differently when they become plural. These are *irregular nouns* (see the list below).

Change the end of the word.

child	children
ox	oxen

Change *f* and *fe* to *ve* and add *s*.

shelf	shelves
elf	elves
thief	thieves
leaf	leaves
loaf	loaves
calf	calves
wolf	wolves
half	halves

sheaf	sheaves
life	lives
knife	knives
wife	wives

Exception: fife, fifes

Add *s* to words ending with a vowel and *o*.

cameo	cameos
cuckoo	cuckoos
igloo	igloos
radio	radios

Add *es* to most words ending with a consonant and *o*.

echo	echoes
hero	heroes
potato	potatoes
tomato	tomatoes

Exceptions: burros, broncos, condos, gizmos, photos, torsos

Add *s* to words that end with *o* and have to do with music.

alto	altos	piano	pianos
banjo	banjos	piccolo	piccolos
cello	cellos	soprano	sopranos
mezzo	mezzos	solo	solos
		tango	tangos

Some words that end with *o* have more than one plural spelling (-os or -oes).

domino	dominos, dominoes
gazebo	gazebos, gazeboes
halo	halos, haloes
mosquito	mosquitos, mosquitoes
motto	mottos, mottoes
tornado	tornados, tornadoes
volcano	volcanos, volcanoes
zero	zeros, zeroes

When a word ends in *y*, change the *y* to *i* and add *es* when the letter before the *y* is a consonant.

baby	babies
lady	ladies
berry	berries
belly	bellies
baby	babies
buggy	buggies
puppy	puppies
guppy	guppies

Exceptions: Proper nouns that end with a consonant and *y* just add *s* to become plural.

Germany	Germanys
Sally	Sallys
Kennedy	Kennedys

Change the middle of the word.

tooth	teeth
mouse	mice
louse	lice
goose	geese
foot	feet
tooth	teeth
man	men

Exceptions:

talisman	talismans
ottoman	ottomans

Family members

mother-in-law	mothers-in-law
father-in-law	fathers-in-law
brother-in-law	brothers-in-law
sister-in-law	sisters-in-law

Add *es* to words that end with the letters *s*, *ss*, *x*, *ch*, and *sh*.

box	boxes
brush	brushes
church	churches
gas	gases
kiss	kisses

Words that don't change from singular to plural

moose	swine
deer	bison
sheep	series

Words with more than one way to spell the plural

fish	fish or fishes
hippopotamus	hippopotami or hippopotamuses
octopus	octopi or octopuses
appendix	appendixes or appendices
wharf	wharfs or wharves
staff	staves (sticks or in music), staffs
person	persons or people
scarf	scarfs or scarves
bus	buses or busses
cactus	cacti or cactuses
hoof	hoofs or hooves
rhinoceros	rhinoceros or rhinoceroses

Words from Latin and Greek

datum	data
medium	media
basis	bases
alga	algae
bacterium	bacteria
crisis	crises
die	dice
alumnus	alumni

8. Adding prefixes

When you add a prefix to a word, don't change the spelling of either the prefix or the word. This is the easiest spelling rule of them all. A prefix is a little part of a word—usually just two to four letters—that you put at the beginning. If you follow this rule, you will never misspell *misspell*, which has two *s's*: one at the end of *mis* and one at the beginning of *spell*.

A prefix always changes the meaning of a word.

Prefix	Base word	Final spelling
anti-	war	antiwar
auto-	biography	autobiography
bi-	cycle	bicycle
co-	operate	cooperate
dis-	appoint	disappoint
il-	legal	illegal
im-	mature	immature
inter-	national	international
ir-	responsible	irresponsible
mid-	term	midterm
mis-	understand	misunderstand
multi-	purpose	multipurpose
non-	essential	nonessential
pre-	view	preview
re-	appear	reappear
tele-	scope	telescope
un-	usual	unusual
under-	ground	underground

Sometimes you have to put a hyphen between the prefix and the base word. See *Hyphens* on page 118.

The only case in which a prefix does not change the meaning of the word it's attached to is inflammable, which you might think means not flammable. Surprise! Inflammable has the same meaning as flammable: easily set on fire and able to burn quickly.

9. Adding Suffixes

Suffixes are little parts of words (like *-ly*, *-ness*, *-ful*, and many more) that go at the end. Usually suffixes change the meanings of words or add information to them.

When you add a suffix to a base word, in most cases you just add it without changing the spelling of the suffix or the base (unless there's a silent *e* at the end of the base word or you have to double the final consonant).

Base	Suffix	Final spelling
adult	-hood	adulthood
appoint	-ment	appointment
back	-ward	backward
beautiful	-ly	beautifully
character	-ize	characterize
cheerful	-ness	cheerfulness

child	-like	childlike
child	-ish	childish
count	-ess	countess
fear	-less	fearless
fraud	-ulent	fraudulent
free	-dom	freedom
govern	-ess	governess
hope	-ful	hopeful
paint	-er	painter
pilgrim	-age	pilgrimage
quarrel	-some	quarrelsome
swordsman	-ship	swordsmanship

See *The silent e. Drop it? Keep it?* on page 51 and *Double the final consonant* on page 55.

10. Silent letters

It would be tough enough to spell English words if you could pronounce all the letters in all the words. But many words contain letters that you don't even sound out when you say them. You still have to put them in when you write them, however. Here are some of the most common words with silent letters.

align, benign, design, sign

answer

balk, caulk, chalk, stalk, talk, walk

bright, flight, light, might, night, right, sight, tight

column

Connecticut

could, should, would

cupboard

debris

dumb, thumb, plumber

gnome

handkerchief, handsome

high, nigh, sigh, thigh

island

knave, knew, knot, know

listen, often

salmon

subtle

thought, brought, taught

Wednesday

wrap, wreck, write, wrong

For more on silent letters, see *Watch out for those first few letters* on page 76.

11. -able or -ible?

Hundreds of words in English end with the letters *-able* or *-ible*, and there's no good rule that will help you decide which ending to put on which word. It's not sens**ible** to have no rule. Really incred**ible**! Unbeliev**able**. And trying to spell words like these can be formid**able** and make you miser**able**. You might think that these words are horr**ible**. Detest**able**. But you are cap**able** of spelling them correctly. You have to. They're unavoid**able**. And it's not accept**able** to spell them wrong. It's inexcus**able**. It's definitely poss**ible** to spell them right. The best thing to do is become familiar with the valu**able** lists below and always check your dictionary or spell-checker when in doubt. That's an attain**able** goal.

-able	-ible
acceptable	accessible
amiable	combustible
attainable	contemptible
avoidable	corruptible
believable	credible
capable	crucible
delectable	edible
deplorable	flexible
desirable	forcible
detestable	horrible
immovable	illegible
inconceivable	impossible
incurable	incredible
inexcusable	indelible
inflammable	inflexible
interchangeable	intangible
invaluable	invincible

justifiable	invisible
miserable	irresponsible
mutable	permissible
notable	plausible
passable	possible
portable	sensible
presentable	tangible
probable	terrible
reliable	visible
respectable	

12. Add *k* to verbs ending with *c*.

When you add -*ing* or -*ed* to some verbs that end with *c*, you have to add *k* first.

So first you *picnic* on the grass. Then you are *picnicking* on the grass. And finally you *picnicked* on the grass.

Here is a list of verbs that end in *c* and add *k* before -*ing* and -*ed*.

Now we . . .	We are . . .	Then we . . .
frolic	frolicking	frolicked
mimic	mimicking	mimicked
panic	panicking	panicked
picnic	picnicking	picnicked
traffic	trafficking	trafficked

13. -*ful* has only one *l*.

Since *beautiful* means "full of beauty" and powerful means "full of power," it is natural to think that these words should end with -*full*. But that is not so. The correct suffix is spelled -*ful*.

The only word in the English language that ends with -*full* is *full*. Below is a list of the most common words that end with -*ful*.

armful	dutiful	helpful	sorrowful
artful	earful	hopeful	spiteful
awful	eventful	hurtful	tablespoonful
bashful	eyeful	joyful	tactful
beautiful	faithful	masterful	tasteful
blissful	fanciful	merciful	teaspoonful
boastful	fateful	mindful	thimbleful
bountiful	fearful	painful	trustful
capful	forceful	peaceful	unlawful
careful	gleeful	pitiful	wasteful
cheerful	graceful	plentiful	wishful
colorful	grateful	powerful	woeful
cupful	handful	shameful	wonderful
doubtful	harmful	sinful	worshipful
dreadful	hateful	skillful	youthful

14. -*ough* is tough!

One group of letters needs a section all its own: -*ough*.

Probably no other combination of four letters in the whole English language has so many different possible pronunciations, and not one of them is "o-ug-huh," as someone might think.

"uff"	"ow"	"off"	"oh"	"aw"	"oo"
enough	bough	cough	although	bought	through
rough	drought	trough	borough	brought	
tough	plough		dough	fought	"up"
			furlough	sought	hiccough
			thorough	thought	
			though	wrought	

Slough can be pronounced three different ways, depending on what the word means.

Slough ("Slow"): A suburb of London, England.

slough ("sloo" and "slow"): A depression, usually filled with deep mud; a stagnant swamp or marsh.

slough ("sluff"): The dead outer skin shed by a reptile or an amphibian.

Now you know how tough ough is.

15. Words with different spellings

Andrew Jackson (1767–1845), the seventh president of the United States, was once trying to write an important paper, and he was having trouble with his spelling. It was reported that he cried out angrily, "It's a poor mind that can think of only one way to spell a word."

In fact, there are many words that have two correct spellings. In your dictionary, you'll see both accepted spellings with the words *or* or *also* between them.

Many words in English that end with *-or* in the United States end with *-our* in Canada and Great Britain (England, Scotland, Northern Ireland, and Wales). People there speak and write English too. In your dictionary, *colour* may be identified as "Chiefly British. Variant of color." (*Variant* means a different, acceptable spelling.)

In the United States, spell the following words with *-or* at the end:

behavior	humor
candor	labor
clamor	misdemeanor
color	neighbor
endeavor	odor
flavor	parlor
harbor	rumor
honor	vigor

Don't be surprised, however, if you sometimes see these words spelled with *-our* at the end, especially in a book or an article by a British writer. (Words that end with *-ize* or *-er* in the United States are sometimes spelled with *-ise* and *-re* in Great Britain. Examples: *apologize, apologise; center, centre.*)

Other words that have two acceptable spellings are

catalogue, catalog

judgement, judgment

theater, theatre

cancellation, cancelation

16. Watch out for those first few letters.

Sometimes you have a better chance of spelling a word right if you can figure out the first few letters. Then at least you'll know where to look in your dictionary.

Since so many English words come from foreign languages, and since there are a lot of silent letters in English, the first few letters of many words are really tricky. The lists below should help you with some of the trickiest.

c sounds like *s* at the beginning of words that start with *ce-*, *ci-*, and *cy-*, like these:

ceiling	censor	ceremony	cinema
celebrate	centigrade	certain	circle
celery	centipede	certify	citizen
cellular	century	cider	citrus
cement	ceramic	cinch	civilization

c sounds like *k* at the beginning of all words that start with *ca-*, *co-*, or *cu-*.

cabin	cobra	cube
cactus	coconut	cuckoo
cadet	code	cuddle
café	coffee	cuff
capital	cog	culprit
cat	cold	cup

ch sounds like *k* at the beginning of words like

character	chord
chemical	chorus
chemistry	Christmas
chlorine	chrome
choral	chronology

ch sounds like *sh* at the beginning of words like

chalet	charade	chauffeur	chiffon
champagne	charlatan	chef	chivalry
chandelier	chateau	chic	chute

g sounds like *j* at the beginning of words like

gelatin	genetic	geometric	gibberish
gem	genie	geranium	gigantic
gender	genius	gerbil	giraffe
gene	gentle	germ	gym
general	gentleman	German	gymnastic
generator	genuine	gesture	gypsy
generosity	geography	giant	gyroscope

gh sounds like *g* at the beginning of words like

Ghana	gherkin	ghost
ghastly	ghetto	ghoul

kn sounds like *n* at the beginning of words like

knack	kneel	knob	know
knapsack	knickerbockers	knock	knowledge

knave	knife	knoll	known
knead	knight	knot	Knox (Fort)
knee	knit	knothole	knuckle

ph sounds like **f** at the beginning of words like

phantom	Philadelphia	phonics
pharmacist	philanthropy	phony
pharmacy	philharmonic	photocopy
pharaoh	philosopher	photography
phase	philosophy	phrase
pheasant	phobia	physical
phenomenal	phone	physician
		physics

ps sounds like **s** at the beginning of words like

| psalm | psoriasis | psychic |
| pseudonym | psychiatrist | psychology |

qu sounds like **kw** at the beginning of words like

quake	quarter	quick	quite
quality	queen	quiet	quiz
quarrel	quench	quilt	quota
quart	question	quit	quote

squ sounds like **skw** at the beginning of words like

| squabble | squash | squeeze |
| squad | squat | squelch |

squadron	squawk	squint
squall	squeak	squirm
squalor	squeal	squirrel
squander	squeamish	squirt
square	squib	squish

wh sounds like *h* at the beginning of words like

| who | whom | whose | who's |

wh sounds like *w* at the beginning of words like

whack	when	whimper	white
whale	where	whip	whittle
wharf	whether	whir	whiz
what	which	whirl	whoops
wheat	whiff	whirlpool	whopper
wheedle	whiffle	whisker	why
wheel	while	whisper	
wheeze	whim	whistle	

wr sounds like *r* at the beginning of words like

wrack	wren	wrinkle	wreckage
wrangle	wrench	wrist	wring
wrap	wrestle	write	
wreath	wretched	wrong	
wreck	wriggle	wrote	

17. Use your dictionary or spell-checker.

When you are writing something and you come to a word that you are not sure how to spell, you can do one of three things:

1. Try to spell it the best you can. Take a wild guess. You might actually get it right. Or you might end up with a sentence like "It wuz a kold and winndy nite."

2. Shout out to the nearest intelligent person, "How do you spell *sarcophagus*?" and hope that he or she is a better speller than you are.

3. Look the word up in your dictionary, or if you are on your computer, use the spell-checker. (Be careful of homonyms! See page 48.)

Don't be a spell-wrecker. Be a spell-checker! Make this your slogan for better spelling:
When in doubt,
get the dictionary out!

CHAPTER FOUR

Capitalization

Capital letters are very handy. They tell us when sentences begin. They identify the names of specific people, places, and things. They're helpful in other ways, too. Here's when to use capital letters and when not to.

Always capitalize the first word of a sentence.

Giraffes would make cute pets if they could fit into the house.

Always capitalize the first word of a direct quote.

I told my teacher, "My pet giraffe ate my homework," but she didn't believe me.

Do not capitalize the first word in an indirect quotation.

I told my teacher that my pet giraffe had eaten my homework, but she didn't believe me.

See *Direct Quotations* on page 122.

Always capitalize the first word of each line of poetry.

"To My Baby Brother, with Love"

On my cookie, you may nibble;

On my drawings, you may scribble;

With these things I will not quibble,

But on my homework, do not dribble.

Thank you.

Always capitalize the pronoun *I*.

I took the bus, and I went to my grandmother's house, and I helped her paint the living room, and I practiced karate with her, and I walked her alligator, and I jogged with her around the park, and I was exhausted.

Do not capitalize the other pronouns (you, he, she, it, we, they, me, him, her, us, them, my, mine, your, yours, his, hers, its, our, ours, their, and theirs) unless they are the first words in a sentence, direct quote, or title.

See *Pronouns* on page 26.

Always capitalize names of specific people.

Karen, David, Jennifer, George Washington, Pookey

Do not capitalize *man*, *woman*, *boy*, *girl*, or other general words that indicate kinds of people without giving their specific names. Always capitalize names of specific places.

Chelsea, MA

Brooklyn

Mississippi River

Pacific Ocean

California

Rocky Mountains

Asia

Central Park

Do not capitalize general place words like *city*, *state*, *mountain*, *river*, and *park* without the specific names in front. Always capitalize specific buildings, monuments, and sites.

the Lincoln Memorial

Statue of Liberty

Golden Gate Bridge

the Kremlin

Empire State Building

Eiffel Tower

the Taj Mahal

Buckingham Palace

Do not capitalize *building*, *statue*, *tower*, **and general words like those without the specific proper nouns in front. Also, do not capitalize the word** *the* **in front of specific buildings or sites unless it is the first word in the sentence, title, or direct quote.**

We took a tour of the White House, but the president wasn't in. So we went to the Washington Monument to see if Washington was there.

Always capitalize organizations and institutions.

Chamber of Commerce

Library of Congress

Smithsonian Institute

Salvation Army

National Football League

Better Business Bureau

Asia Society

Do not capitalize general words like *library*, *institute*, **and** *society* **without the specific names in front.**

Always capitalize sports teams.

Atlanta Braves

Dallas Mavericks

Chicago Bears

Anaheim Ducks

Do not capitalize general words like *team*, *club*, **or** *group* **without the specific names.**

Always capitalize schools and colleges.

Columbia Prep School

Tufts University

Brooklyn College

State University of New York at New Paltz

Do not capitalize *school*, *college*, *university*, **and general words like those without the names in front.**

Always capitalize proper adjectives.

French poodle, French fries, French horn, Chinese food, German measles, Italian fashions, Japanese technology, Indian restaurant, Russian dances, Swiss cheese, Belgian lace, American economy

Proper adjectives are made from proper nouns.
See Proper Nouns on page 12.

Always capitalize initials that are part of someone's name.

C. S. Lewis, J. R. R. Tolkien, John F. Kennedy,
F.D.R. (Franklin Delano Roosevelt), J. K. Rowling

Always capitalize official titles or positions when used with names.

General Kilmer, Captain Millan, President Obama, King Tut,
Prime Minister Cameron, Chairman Mao

Do not capitalize *captain*, *general*, *ambassador*, **and similar general words without the names.**

Always capitalize family members when used with their names.

Uncle George, Aunt Roz, Grandma Karen, Cousin Cindy

Do not capitalize *uncle*, *aunt*, *grandpa*, **and general family words like those without the names except when you are using the titles of family members in place of their names.**

Always capitalize *Mom*, *Dad*, *Grandma*, *Auntie*, **etc., when used as if they were names.**

Grandma told Mom that Dad had said to tell Grandpa that Auntie should meet him where he had told her to. Understand?

Do not capitalize *mom*, *dad*, *grandpa*, **or similar family titles after** *my*, *your*, *his*, **or similar possessive words.**

My mom and her dad used to go to college together.

Always capitalize family members when used as nouns of direct address.

And now, Mom, Dad, Grandma, and Grandpa, sit down and listen, because I have some astounding news to tell you.

See *Noun of Direct Address* on page 17.

Always capitalize the days of the week.

Tuesday, Thursday, Saturday

Always capitalize the months of the year.

February, April, July, August

Do not capitalize the seasons of the year.

spring, summer, fall, autumn, winter

Exceptions: If the name of the season is the first word in a sentence, a word in a title, or part of the name of a local holiday, it should be capitalized.

My favorite poem is "Spring Has Sprung."

Winter is harsh in the Arctic regions. Ask a polar bear.

Decorations for the Super Summer Carnival were super.

This year our show is called "Fashions for Fall."

Always capitalize the first word in the salutation (greeting) of a friendly letter.

Hi, everyone,

Dearest friend,

Greetings,

Dear Dr. Sen,

Always capitalize the first word, the last word, and all important words in the salutation (greeting) of a business letter.

Dear Customer Relations Department:

Dear Public Safety Commissioner:

Dear Chairman of the Board:

Always capitalize the first word in the closing of a letter.

Yours truly,	Sincerely yours,	Respectfully and gratefully,
Best wishes,	Warmest regards,	Farewell for now,

Always capitalize the first word, the last word, and all the main words in titles of

Books— *Harry Potter and the Deathly Hallows*

Movies— *How to Train Your Dragon*

Songs— "You Light Up My Life"

Plays or musicals— *Beauty and the Beast*

Magazines— *Science World*

Newspapers— the *Los Angeles Times*

TV Shows— *A Charlie Brown Christmas*

Do not capitalize small words in a title, like *a*, *an*, *the*, *in*, **or** *to* **unless they're the first or last words.**

Always capitalize school subjects when they are the names of languages or specific courses listed in the school catalog.

French Literature   Introduction to Swahili

Psychology for Beginners   World History II

Advanced Biology   Mastering Mathematics

Do not capitalize subjects that are not the names of languages or specific courses: *mathematics*, *geography*, *history*, *science*, **etc.**

Always capitalize the first word of each line of an outline.

I. The world's weirdest people
    A. Weird men
        1. Appearance
        2. Actions
        3. Occupations
    B. Weird women
        1. Names
        2. Hairdos
        3. Clothing

Always capitalize geographic locations when they refer to specific areas on the map.

She was born in the East, moved to the West when she was nine, traveled throughout the Northwest after college, and finally settled in the South. She's been around!

Do not capitalize *north, east, south, west,* **etc., when they mean directions, not locations.**

I was supposed to drive three miles south and then turn west. Instead, I drove eight miles north and then turned east. No wonder I was late for the party.

Always capitalize national holidays.

Thanksgiving, Father's Day, Labor Day, Memorial Day, Washington's Birthday, Martin Luther King, Jr. Day, New Year's Day

Always capitalize religious holidays.

Christmas, Easter, Eid el-Fitr, Rosh Hashanah, Saint Patrick's Day

Always capitalize local holidays, festivals, and special events.

Young Authors Conference, Reading Rodeo, Winter Wonderland, Fall Festival, Back-to-School Fair, Kiddie Carnival

Do not capitalize words like *festival*, *jubilee*, and *carnival* when they don't have specific names with them.

Always capitalize races, nationalities, and religions.

Caucasian, Semitic, Belgian, Italian, Spanish, Africans, Arabic, Christianity, Judaism, Asians, Muslims

Always capitalize languages.

French, Hebrew, Japanese, Latin, Greek, Russian

Always capitalize historical periods, documents, wars, and events.

the Great Depression
Declaration of Independence
the Battle of Bunker Hill

the Iraq War
the Middle Ages
the Renaissance

Do not capitalize general words like *war*, *battle*, or *treaty* without specific names.

Always capitalize gods and goddesses.

God, Savior, Buddha, Jehovah, Allah, Jupiter, Venus, Aphrodite

Do not capitalize the words *god* and *goddess* used in a general way.

People in ancient times believed that gods and goddesses could reward them if they were good.

Always capitalize the word *Bible* (Old and New Testaments) and all books of the Bible.

Bible, Genesis, Proverbs, Revelation, Matthew

Always capitalize religious books.

the Koran, the Torah, the New Testament, Scriptures

Always capitalize the names of the planets.

Mercury, Venus, Mars, Jupiter

Do not capitalize *sun* and *moon*. Capitalize *Earth* when it refers to the third planet from the sun, our specific planet. When *earth* means dirt or soil, it is not capitalized.

Always capitalize the first word in a long sentence after a colon.

There was a sign on the front door: There is no school today, because the principal has gone fishing!

Do not capitalize the first word in a list after a colon.

Stuff to take to the party: pretzels, my goldfish, CDs, DVDs, my favorite pillow, and jelly-flavored toothpaste.

Always capitalize abbreviations of a title after someone's name.

John Smith, Jr.   Mortimore Snobly, Sr.

Wellman Sickly, M.D.   Henry Brainy, Ph.D.

Always capitalize A.M. and P.M.—or, don't.
A.M. (*ante meridiem*, before noon) and P.M. (*post meridiem*, after noon) can be capitalized or not. People do it both ways. It's your choice, but once you decide, do it the same way all the time.

Both are correct: 5:30 A.M. and 5:30 a.m.

Always capitalize A.D. and B.C.

Julius Caesar was assassinated in 44 B.C.
In A.D. 1492, Columbus set sail over the ocean blue.

Note that A.D. comes before the year and B.C. comes after the year.

Always capitalize the U.S. Postal Service abbreviations for the states.

Alabama: AL	Massachusetts: MA	South Dakota: SD
Alaska: AK	Michigan: MI	Tennessee: TN
Arizona: AZ	Minnesota: MN	Texas: TX
Arkansas: AR	Mississippi: MS	Utah: UT
California: CA	Missouri: MO	Vermont: VT
Colorado: CO	Montana: MT	Virginia: VA
Connecticut: CT	Nebraska: NE	Washington: WA
Delaware: DE	Nevada: NV	West Virginia: WV
Florida: FL	New Hampshire: NH	Wisconsin: WI
Georgia: GA	New Jersey: NJ	Wyoming: WY
Hawaii: HI	New Mexico: NM	
Idaho: ID	New York: NY	
Illinois: IL	North Carolina: NC	
Indiana: IN	North Dakota: ND	
Iowa: IA	Ohio: OH	
Kansas: KS	Oklahoma: OK	
Kentucky: KY	Oregon: OR	
Louisiana: LA	Pennsylvania: PA	
Maine: ME	Rhode Island: RI	
Maryland: MD	South Carolina: SC	

Always capitalize names of products.

Nintendo games, New Balance sneakers, Cheerios, Kleenex tissues, Jell-O pudding

Do not capitalize general words like *sneakers, cereal, tissues,* **and** *pudding.*

Always capitalize names of companies.

Sony Corporation, General Motors, Kellogg Company, Parker Brothers

Punctuation

WHY YOU NEED PROPER PUNCTUATION

Without proper punctuation, it would be hard to read what you've written. Punctuation marks are like little road signs that tell you when to slow down, pause, and stop as you read. They group phrases and clauses together. They help writers show their feelings and get their messages across clearly.

So it's very important for you to use perfectly proper punctuation whenever you can. Otherwise your writing might be confusing. And no reader wants to read confusing writing.

Apostrophes

CONTRACTIONS

An apostrophe takes the place of the missing letter(s) in a contraction.

A contraction is a word you make by putting two or more words together and leaving out one or more letters.

Here are some contractions that you use every day.

aren't	doesn't	he'd
can't	don't	he'll
could've	hadn't	he's
couldn't	hasn't	I'd
didn't	haven't	I'll
I'm	shouldn't	we've
I've	they'd	weren't
isn't	they'll	who'd
it's	they're	who'll
let's	they've	who's
might've	wasn't	won't
she'd	we'd	would've
she'll	we'll	wouldn't
she's	we're	you've

Contractions can sometimes be tricky, so be careful about the following:

The *'ve* at the end of *should've*, *could've*, and *would've* always stands for *have*, never for *of*. For instance, *should've* means *should have*, not *should of*.

You're (a contraction) means *you are*.
Your (a possessive pronoun) means *belongs to you*.
You're wrong if you think that your smelly dog is going to sleep in my bed.

It's (a contraction) stands for two words: *it is* or *it has*.

Its (a possessive pronoun) means *belongs to it*.

What's the gerbil doing? It's eating its dinner. (It is eating the dinner that belongs to it.)

Let's (a contraction) means *let us*.

Lets is the present tense of the verb *to let*.

Sometimes Lexi lets us eat bugs, so let's ask her if we can do it today.

Who's (a contraction) means *who is* or *who has*.

Whose (a possessive pronoun) means *belongs to whom*.

Whose mess is this, and who's going to clean it up? (Who does this mess belong to, and who is going to clean it up?)

POSSESSIVE NOUNS

Use apostrophes in all possessive nouns.

One of the jobs that nouns do in sentences is show possession or ownership. Every possessive noun must have an apostrophe. Sometimes it comes before the *s* at the end, and sometimes it comes after it. How do you know when to use *'s* and when to use *s'* ? It's easier than you think.

SINGULAR POSSESSIVE NOUNS

If the noun is singular, add *'s* to make it possessive.

It doesn't matter what the last letter of the singular noun is. It could be *s* or even *ss*. Just add *'s* to all singular nouns to make them show ownership.

Dennis's ladder
the chipmunk's nuts
my boss's lamp shade
Andrew's helicopter

There is one possible exception to this rule: when you make the names of people from ancient literature, mythology, or the Bible possessive. If their names end with *s*, you can add either *'s* or just an apostrophe: Moses' orders, Jesus' sermon, Aeneas' ship, Odysseus' bow, Hercules' feats. If the name ends with any letter besides *s*, follow the regular rule for singular possessive nouns: add *'s*.

PLURAL POSSESSIVE NOUNS

If the noun is plural and you want it to show possession, look at the last letter.

If the last letter of a plural noun is *s*, add an apostrophe to make it possessive.

the baseball players' uniforms
the musicians' instruments
the Leongs' house
the elephants' watering hole

If the last letter of a plural noun is not *s*, add *'s* to make it possessive.

Most plural nouns end with *s*, but there are some irregular nouns that don't. Here are a few.

the women's briefcases
the mice's cheese
the fathers-in-law's gifts
the children's toys

Remember:
- Every possessive noun must have an apostrophe.
- All singular possessive nouns end with *'s*.
- If the last letter of a plural noun is *s*, just add an apostrophe to make it possessive.
- If the last letter of a plural noun is not *s*, add *'s* to make it possessive.

PLURALS OF LETTERS, SIGNS, WORDS, AND SYMBOLS

Use *'s* to make letters, signs, words, and symbols plural.

How many *a*'s are there in *Afghanistan*?

Don't put too many !'s at the end of your sentences, or you'll sound too hysterical.

Instead of using so many *very*'s in your story, try other adverbs like *extremely* or *intensely*.

She drew :-)'s all over her bedroom wall.

Apostrophes are really important when you make letters plural to avoid confusion in a sentence like this:

Mississippi is spelled with four is, four ss, and two ps.

See how much easier it is to read with the apostrophes:

Mississippi is spelled with four i's, four s's, and two p's.

Brackets

Use brackets to add your own words to words you are quoting.

"We hold these truths to be self-evident, that all men [and all women, too, if you ask me] are created equal."

—The Declaration of Independence

Use brackets around your words that replace someone else's words that you cut out to make a quotation shorter.

Original version:

Dear Editor:

I am so distressed that the city is going to take over our community garden, that when the bulldozers come to knock down the beeches, birches, cedars, cherries, chestnuts, maples, oaks, pines, and poplars, I'm going to chain myself to the gate and not let them in.

Sincerely,
The Leaf Lady

Shortened version with brackets around one word that was inserted to replace ten words that were deleted:

Dear Editor:

I am so distressed that the city is going to take over our community garden, that when the bulldozers come to knock down the . . . [trees], I'm going to chain myself to the gate and not let them in.

Sincerely,
The Leaf Lady

See *Ellipses* on page 113 to see what the three dots in the letter above mean.

Use brackets around *sic* to keep someone's mistake when you quote his or her words.

Sic is a Latin word that means *just so*. When you quote someone who has made a mistake, and you don't correct the mistake in the quote, put *sic* after the mistake. It is usually italicized (slants to the right) and in brackets (though sometimes parentheses can be used). The reader will know that what comes before [*sic*] is spelled wrong or is an error of fact.

He wrote that the song begins, "My country 'tis of thee, sweet land of liver tea [*sic*], of thee I sing."

Some people put stage directions in brackets when they write the script of a play. The brackets separate what the actor says from what he or she does.

Roslyn: [stomping her foot on the floor] Keep those pigs out of my kitchen!

Colons

Use a colon after a full sentence that introduces a list.

> For your geography test, memorize the names and locations of the five longest rivers in the world: Nile (Africa), Amazon (South America), Yangtze (Asia), Mississippi-Missouri (North America), and Yenisey-Angara (Asia).

For special effect, just one item, not a whole list, can come after a colon.

> I forgot to pack the most important thing for the picnic: bug spray!

Do not use a colon after any words that are part of the verb *to be* (am, are, is, was, were, be, being, been).

> The names of the deserts of Africa are Arabian, Kalahari, Libyan, Namib, Nubian, and Sahara.

Use a colon after headings in a memo and after the greeting of a business letter.

To: Mrs. R. Penn
From: Mrs. L. Freedman
Date: April 28, 2011
Subject: Toy Designs
Dear Chairman of the Board:

Use a colon to separate the volume number from the page number of a book, magazine, or newspaper.

The Encyclopedia of Animals X:814 (That means volume 10, page 814.)

Use a colon to separate the number of the chapter from the number of the verse in the books of the Bible.

Luke 2:7 (That means chapter two, verse seven.)

Use a colon to separate hours from minutes.

3:25 p.m.   6:20 a.m.

Use a colon to separate the parts of a ratio.

The diagram is drawn on a scale of 60:1.

Use a colon to separate a heading from what follows.

DANGER: MAN-EATING GUPPIES SWIM IN THIS RIVER!

Use a colon to separate the title of a book from its subtitle.

Pigs in My Kitchen: Life on a Farm

Some writers use a colon in a script of a play to separate the name of a character from what he or she says.

Roslyn: Keep those pigs out of my kitchen!

Commas

Join two independent clauses with a comma and a conjunction.

See *Compound Sentence* on page 41.

Shana lives in Massachusetts, and her sister Sasha lives in Florida.

Put commas between three or more independent clauses if they don't already have commas in them.

See *Independent Clause* on page 40.

David does digital retouching on his computer, Jennifer designs original jewelry, and Karen is a special education teacher.

Put a comma after a dependent clause that comes before an independent clause in a complex sentence.

See *Clauses* on page 40 and *Complex Sentence* on page 41.

Because it's my granddaughter's birthday, I'm dressing like a clown for her party.

Put a comma between adjectives that describe the same noun.

See *Adjectives* on page 21.

He wore an amazing, astounding, fantastic clown costume to his granddaughter's party.

Put a comma after a prepositional phrase that does the job of an adverb.

See *Prepositional Phrases* on page 25 and *Adverbs* on page 23.

Underneath the rotting floorboards in the creaky cabin, Mistress Margo found Captain Bill's secret treasure chest.

> If the prepositional phrase is very short, you can skip the comma.
>
> After today Max will be the duke of North Conway.

Put commas around phrases and clauses that give information but are not necessary to get the main meaning of the sentence across.

These phrases and clauses are called *nonrestrictive*. They could be deleted from the sentence without changing the main meaning of the sentence.

In 1828 the city of Philadelphia, which is in Pennsylvania, tried to sell the Liberty Bell for scrap metal.

Put a comma after *yes*, *no*, *oh*, and similar mild interjections at the beginnings of sentences.

Oh, I didn't know Isla was under the basket.

Yes, Hayden jumped into the fountain to get Callie's lucky penny back.

No, I won't wear a pickle costume to the wedding.

Put an exclamation point after an interjection that shows strong feelings. See *Interjections* on page 29.

Put a comma after the greeting of a personal letter and after the close of a personal or business letter.

My dear Mrs. Konikowski,	Dear George,
Hello, Glenn and Laurie,	Yours truly,
Sincerely,	Love,

Use a comma to make the reader pause slightly to avoid possible confusion in understanding the meaning of a sentence.

Confusing: Immediately before the flying fish flew away.

Clear: Immediately before, the flying fish flew away.

Use a comma to separate two words that are the same in a sentence.

When his hand went up up flew the flag.
When his hand went up, up flew the flag.

After the cat came in in skated my sister.
After the cat came in, in skated my sister.

Use commas to separate three or more items in a series.

Ellen, Fran, Peter, Bonnie, Sandra, Barbara, Miriam, Mark, Chris, and Lucy are all members of my "Make the World Better" group.

Use a comma in front of a direct quotation that does not begin a sentence.

> Ms. Markovits announced, "The trip to Boston has been postponed because the bus broke down."

See *Quotation Marks* on page 122.

Use a comma at the end of the first part of a direct quotation that is broken up in a sentence.

> "Come to my house for lunch," Lorraine told Rozzie, "but please leave your gorilla at home, because it scares my goldfish."

Use a comma before the second part of a direct quotation that is broken up in a sentence.

> "I can't leave my gorilla at home alone," said Rozzie to Lorraine, "because he's afraid to be by himself."

Put a comma after the last word of a direct quotation that is a declarative sentence unless the last word of the direct quotation is the last word of the whole sentence.

> "Well, maybe your gorilla and my goldfish can be friends," said Lorraine to Rozzie.

See *Declarative Sentence* on page 32.

If the last word of a direct quotation is the last word of the whole sentence, put the appropriate punctuation mark after it (period, question mark, or exclamation point) followed by quotation marks.

Said Lorraine to Rozzie, "Well, maybe your gorilla and my goldfish can be friends."

Put a comma after a noun of direct address that begins a sentence.

Bonnie, please tell Kurt that his parakeet got an e-mail.

See *Noun of Direct Address* on page 17.

Put a comma before a noun of direct address that ends a sentence.

Please remind Dennis to pick up the coconuts, Lynda.

Put commas around a noun of direct address that is in the middle of a sentence.

When Phoenix gets home, Archer, he'll help you with your homework.

Use one or two commas to set off appositives and official titles. See *Appositive* on page 19.

William Jefferson Clinton, the forty-second president of the United States, was known as just Bill, and James Earl Carter, the thirty-ninth president, was known as just Jimmy.

Use commas to set off little expressions that break the flow of thought

in a sentence.

Mrs. Potter, after all, is the dean.

Use a comma before and after abbreviations like *e.g.* and *i.e.* and words like *namely*.

e.g. are the initials of Latin words that mean *for example*.

i.e. are the initials of Latin words that mean *that is to say*.

Sandee was suspended from school for many reasons, e.g., gluing the bathroom doors shut and letting the snakes loose.

Her behavior was considered egregious, i.e., very, very bad.

Use commas to separate parts of an address in a sentence.

They lived at 882 Fifty-first Street, Brooklyn, New York, until they sold the house and moved to 77 Shawmut Street, Chelsea, Massachusetts, in the 1940s.

Use commas to separate parts of a date in the middle of a sentence (including after the year).

The two best dates in their lives were February 14, 1972, and July 19, 1976, because those were the days when their children were born.

If the date has only two parts to it, skip the comma.

Their children were born in February 1972 and July 1976.

Use commas before and after *etc.* in the middle of a sentence.

Since *etc.* is an abbreviation for the Latin phrase *et cetera*, which means *and so forth*, it always has a period after it.

> Barbara and Howard love to travel, shop, spend time with their children, juggle flaming torches, etc., but they have to be careful not to set the house on fire when they juggle the torches.

If *etc.* is the last word in the sentence, don't put a comma after it.

> Jed drives a cab, flies a plane, etc.

Dashes

> On a keyboard, you can type two hyphens to make a dash. The word processing program on your computer might also be able to make an em dash. It's about the length of the letter "m."

When you interrupt your words with a definition, an example, a new fact, or a personal comment and then go on, put a dash before and a dash after the interruption.

> Last Thursday—a marvelous and terrible day—I won the trophy and then broke it.

> The shortest girls on the basketball team—Karen, Marcy, Helene, Harriet, and Caron—always score the highest number of points.

See *Hyphens* on page 116.

Use a dash after a statement that is interrupted or unfinished.

> The principal declared, "The winner of the prize is —" but then the microphone suddenly went dead, so I didn't know if I had won.

Use a dash before the name of a person whose words you are quoting.

> You can fool some of the people all of the time, and all of the people some of the time, but you cannot fool all of the people all of the time.
> —Abraham Lincoln

Use a dash instead of a comma before an appositive to make it more dramatic.

> I dropped the bowl of soup in the lap of Dr. Richard Soghoian—my new boss!

See *Appositive* on page 19.

Ellipses

Ellipsis is singular. Ellipses is plural.

Three dots in a row are called an ellipsis. Use an ellipsis to show where you left words out of a quotation.

Original sentence (thirty-one words):

Most people think that America's total and complete

independence from Great Britain, the mother country across the great Atlantic Ocean, was formally and officially declared on the fourth of July in 1776.

Shortened sentence (seventeen words) with ellipses replacing the words that were cut out:

Most people think that America's . . . independence from Great Britain . . . was . . . declared on the fourth of July in 1776.

Use a period plus an ellipsis (total: four dots) to show that you left words out at the end of a sentence you are quoting.

Original sentence:

The members of the Continental Congress celebrated the event four days later on July 8, 1776, with a big parade, and most delegates didn't sign the Declaration of Independence until August 2, 1776.

Shortened sentence with words cut out at the end:

The members of the Continental Congress celebrated the event four days later on July 8, 1776, with a big parade. . . .

Use a period plus an ellipsis (four dots) to show that you left out a whole sentence or a whole paragraph from a long quotation.

Original paragraph:

Most people think that America's total and complete independence from Great Britain, the mother country across the great Atlantic Ocean, was formally and officially declared on the fourth of July in 1776. That is why today Independence Day is always celebrated with parades and fireworks on the Fourth of July. However, the truth is that the Continental Congress declared the "United Colonies Free and Independent States" on the second of July.

Shortened paragraph with one whole sentence deleted:

Most people think that America's total and complete independence from Great Britain, the mother country across the great Atlantic Ocean, was formally and officially declared on the fourth of July in 1776. . . . However, the truth is that the Continental Congress declared the "United Colonies Free and Independent States" on the second of July.

Use an ellipsis to show exactly where a person hesitated or stopped speaking for a moment.

When John asked Cindy to marry her, she said, "This is such a surprise to . . . I never knew you felt . . . I don't know what to . . . What did you say your name was?"

Exclamation Points

Some people call exclamation points exclamation marks. Both terms are correct.

Put an exclamation point at the end of an exclamatory sentence.

Three juggling seals are performing in the schoolyard right now!

See *Exclamatory Sentence* on page 32.

Put an exclamation point at the end of an imperative sentence that gives a strong order or command.

Stop tickling me!

See *Imperative Sentence* on page 32.

Hyphens

A hyphen is like a dash, but it's shorter. A hyphen goes inside words. A dash goes between words.

Use a hyphen in some compound nouns and in compound adjectives that come in front of the nouns they describe.

Most compound words are written as one word, but some have hyphens, like these:

close-up	all-time	custom-made	able-bodied
life-size	self-made	bad-tempered	

Use a hyphen to make a compound adjective with the prefix *well* when the adjective is used in front of the noun it describes.

well-fed   well-off   well-bred   well-done

well-knit   well-read   well-known   well-meant

well-worn   well-spoken   well-fixed   well-to-do

The well-worn book was on the shelf.

The book on the shelf was well worn.

Use a hyphen between prefixes and proper nouns and adjectives.

all-American values   non-Mongolian foods

anti-Antarctic feelings pro-American rallies

mid-April carnival   un-Elizabethan costumes

Use a hyphen to separate a word into syllables when the word can't fit at the end of a line.

"We have not failed," said Thomas Edison after so many ruined experiments. "We now know a thou-sand things that won't work, so we are much closer to finding what will."

Use a hyphen when you write out numbers from twenty-one to ninety-nine in words. You can write numbers as numerals starting with 101.

thirty-three   fifty-nine   sixty-four

Use a hyphen in fractions written as words.

three-eighths   one-third   four-fifths

Use hyphens when you spell words out for dramatic effect.

You are nuts. Nuts! N-u-t-s. Nuts!

Use a hyphen in double last names.

When Ms. Dilly wed Mr. Dally, their married name was Mr. and Mrs. Dilly-Dally.

Use a hyphen to prevent confusion between words.

recount: to tell a story   re-count: to count again
recollect: to remember   re-collect: to collect again
recover: to get back   re-cover: to cover again

As soon as I recover the use of my broken arm, I'll re-cover the sofa with new upholstery.

Before I recount my adventures with the pirates, let me re-count the number of gold coins in my treasure box.

I can't recollect if I gathered those stamps together, so I'll have to re-collect them.

Use a hyphen after a prefix if the last letter of the prefix is the same as the first letter of the base word.

anti-inflation   pre-election   extra-active   pro-oxidant

Sometimes, if the last letter of the prefix and the first letter of the base word are both vowels, a hyphen goes between them to make the word easier to read. If you're not sure about the hyphen in a specific word, check your dictionary.

pro-education   co-author

See *Adding prefixes* on page 67.

Use a hyphen to mean *to* or *versus* between years, times, numbers, pages, people, and places.

On pages 21-28 in volume C-F, you will read about the famous Chicken-Turkey War (1742-1743) that was fought on the old Chelsea-Brooklyn road. Approximately 40-50 chickens mysteriously disappeared one dark, stormy night from 1-2 a.m. and were never seen again.

Parentheses

Put parentheses around extra words or an extra sentence that you put into your own writing (not something you are quoting) to give additional details, facts, opinions, or explanations.

The newest smartphones (with all the latest apps) are going on sale next Tuesday.

The newest smartphones (I'd love to get one with purple stripes) are going on sale next Tuesday.

Put parentheses around letters or numbers in a list.

> To get into trouble, follow these directions exactly:
> (1) Take off your shoes and socks.
> (2) Wiggle your toes in the mud.
> (3) Go into your house.
> (4) Walk on the newly cleaned kitchen floor.

Put parentheses around a question mark to show that you're not 100 percent sure that a fact is accurate.

> The ballerina lost ninety-three (?) pounds on the seaweed and mashed potatoes diet.

You can put parentheses instead of brackets around stage directions in the script of a play.

> Roslyn: (stomping her foot on the floor) Keep those pigs out of my kitchen!

Periods

Put a period at the end of a declarative sentence (a sentence that states a fact).

> Columbia Grammar and Prep School was founded in 1764.

> See *Declarative Sentence* on page 32.

Put a period at the end of a mild imperative sentence (that gives an order or asks a favor).

Open your books to page twenty-four and answer questions 1, 2, and 1,346.

See *Imperative Sentence* on page 32.

Put a period and a space after an initial in a person's name.

A. A. Milne   W. E. B. DuBois   E. B. White

Put a period after numbers on a list when the items are printed one on top of the other.

What to do on a Saturday morning:
1. Wake up
2. Get out of bed
3. Go to the bathroom
4. Wash your hands
5. Get back into bed
6. Go back to sleep

Put a period after some abbreviations.

A.D.   Prof.   a.m.   B.A.   St.
Ave.   Rd.   Blvd.   M.D.   P.O.

Some abbreviations don't have periods. When in doubt, check your dictionary.

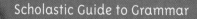

Question Marks

Put a question mark at the end of a sentence that asks a question.

> Is this the famous statue of Sir Cedric the Chicken-Hearted and his favorite pet, Magda the Mouse?

See *Interrogative Sentence* on page 32.

Put a question mark inside a pair of parentheses after a fact, date, or spelling that you're not 100 percent sure of.

> In 2018 (?) a thousand space pioneers will blast off from Nevada (?) to colonize the planet Zizzle.

Don't put a question mark after a mild imperative sentence that sounds like a question but is really a polite request.

> Will you please open that door and see if the monster is still in the closet.

See *Imperative Sentence* on page 32.

Quotation Marks

Put quotation marks around words you are quoting directly in a sentence.

> "I am so happy that you are in my class," announced Mr. Wilson to his smiling Latin students.

Put quotation marks around words that are meant to be sarcastic, mocking, ironic, or surprising, or words that give definitions or explanation.

I didn't know that *repugnant* meant "disgusting" when I called your brother that.

You leaned against the wet paint in your tuxedo? No wonder they call you "genius."

Put quotation marks around the titles of

chapters in a book: "The Scary Toenail"

magazine or newspaper articles: "How to Boil a Turnip"

songs: "Kiss My Tulips with Your Two Lips"

episodes of a TV show: "Summer's First Teeth"

speeches: "What I Learned during Lunch Period in Middle School"

poems: "It's Time to Climb to Rhyme"

Semicolons

Use a semicolon to join two independent clauses in a compound sentence.

Remember:
independent clause + independent clause =
compound sentence

Justin's birthday is on February 3; Amanda's is on December 28.

See *Clauses* on page 39 and *Compound Sentence* on page 41.

Use a semicolon with certain conjunctions or phrases (see list below) in compound sentences.

accordingly	also	as a result
besides	consequently	for example
for instance	for this reason	furthermore
hence	however	in addition
in fact	indeed	moreover
nevertheless	on the contrary	thus
on the other hand	that is	therefore
yet		

He lost his book bag twenty-four times; therefore, his mother glued it to his jacket.

It's snowing and ten degrees below zero; however, I still think we should have the picnic.

Use a semicolon between phrases or clauses in a series that already have commas in them.

At the supermarket I bought bananas, apples, and corn at the produce counter; chicken, hamburger, and bologna at the meat counter; cupcakes, bread, and cookies in the bakery; and paper plates, cups, and napkins in the paper goods section.

Slashes

Put a space-slash-space between lines from a poem when you quote a few lines in a paragraph.

She turned, brushed her hair from her face, and shouted to her dog: "A man who came from Zanzibar / Was playing songs on his guitar / I thought it seemed a bit bizarre / That he would claim he was the czar!" What could the dog say after that?

Put a slash between words that you use in pairs.

neither/nor yes/no hot/cold up/down

Put slashes between parts of an Internet address.

http://www2.scholastic.com/browse/home.jsp

Slashes in Internet addresses are sometimes called *forward slashes*. Colons, periods, and dashes can also be used in Internet addresses.

Underlines

Put an underline under the title of a

book: Harry Potter and the Sorcerer's Stone
play, opera, or musical show: The Lion King
magazine or newspaper: DynaMath, International Herald-Tribune
movie: The Wizard of Oz
radio or television program: Sesame Street

When writing with a computer, you may also put titles into italics (letters that slant to the right like *this*) without underlines if you want to.

CHAPTER SIX

Getting Your Message Across

COMMUNICATING IDEAS

It's great to know about the parts of speech, spelling, punctuation, sentences, and paragraphs. But there's a lot more to communicating what you want to say to your readers in a way that will be interesting, understandable, and lively. You need to know a lot of vocabulary words, words that have the same and opposite meanings, words that can be really tricky, language that is imaginative and poetic, and special expressions and sayings, too.

VOCABULARY

Some word experts estimate that there are over 600,000 words in English, and more are being added all the time. In Shakespeare's day, about 400 years ago, there were only 50,000 words. The language has grown twelve times bigger since then!

But don't feel bad if you don't know what all those words mean. Nobody does, not even the people who write dictionaries. (They always have their own dictionaries nearby to look words up.) The person who knows the most English words (whoever he or she is) probably knows only a small fraction of the total number.

But if you want to be a good writer and get all your ideas across most effectively, you need to build up your vocabulary.

Active and Passive Vocabularies

Everybody has an active vocabulary and a passive vocabulary.

Your active vocabulary contains all the words you use every day when you talk to your parents and friends and when you write letters and e-mails to people.

Your passive vocabulary is much bigger. It contains all the words that you understand if someone else uses them, but that you don't use regularly yourself.

There's also a kind of middle vocabulary, part active and part passive. It contains the words you use when speaking to teachers or other adults and the words you use when writing homework assignments like book reports and research papers.

Learning Vocabulary from Context

Most readers can figure out what a word means, more or less, from context, the words and sentences around it.

For instance, if you read, *"His actions were considered heinous by everyone who knew about them,"* you might not know what *heinous* means. Were his actions good or bad, smart or stupid, funny or serious? But if you read the sentence before or the sentence after, you might be able to make a reasonable guess about the meaning of *heinous*.

He had been in big trouble before, but now he surprised even those who already thought of him as a terrible person. His actions were considered heinous by many people who knew about them. They were furious about what he had done. They could not forgive him. He would have to be punished.

If you guessed, after reading the whole paragraph, that *heinous* means "very bad, wicked, or terrible," you'd be absolutely right. If you carefully read the context of an unfamiliar word, all the words and sentences that surround that word, you can often arrive at a fairly good definition that fits that context.

Use Your Dictionary

Of course, if the context doesn't help, there's always the dictionary.

A good dictionary (in book form, a program on your computer, or downloaded from the Internet) is absolutely essential for any writer.

In addition to the definitions of a word, a good dictionary will tell you how to spell the word, how to pronounce it, what its part of speech is, what other forms the word has, its synonyms and antonyms, where it came from, what expressions it may appear in, and any special information you may need to know about it so that you don't confuse it with other words. That's a lot of important information for a writer.

Let's see how much you can learn from a dictionary about the meaning of a word you already know, *strike*.

strike, v.

1. to hit or attack with the hand or an object (*She struck her little brother on the head with the feather duster.*)

2. to crash into (*The hot-air balloon struck the tree as it flew over.*)

3. to light on fire by scratching (*He strikes a match to light the campfire.*)

4. to indicate time by a sound like a bong or ring (*The clock in the tower struck three.*)

5. to have an effect or make an impression on someone (*It struck the teacher as a good idea not to give homework that day.*)

6. to find, come upon, or discover suddenly (*They struck gold in California in 1849.*)

7. to refuse to work in order to get higher pay or better working conditions (*The workers in the factory voted to strike if they didn't get raises.*)

Were you surprised to find seven different definitions of *strike*? And those were only the verbs. These definitions can be found in a typical school dictionary. One college-level dictionary lists over thirty definitions of the verb *strike*.

There are several other meanings for *strike* when it's used as a noun: *The pitcher threw three strikes and the batter was out. The bowler threw a strike with her very first ball. The air strike destroyed the village. The telephone workers' strike lasted two weeks.*

A good dictionary will also tell you that *struck* is the past tense of the verb, and that the word is used in expressions like "strike out," "strike up the band," "strike it rich," "strike a happy medium," and "strike while the iron is hot."

A good dictionary can give a writer like you a ton of valuable, fascinating information.

How to Build Up Your Vocabulary

Don't let a strange word escape you. When you come upon a new word, circle it, underline it, highlight it — do something to make it stand out. If you can't write on the page, use stick-on notes.

Try to figure out the meaning of the word from its context.

See *Learning Vocabulary from Context* on page 128.

Look the word up in the closest dictionary (in a book or on your computer).

Write the definition down in a handy notebook of new words or on blank flash cards. Later, look over your new words and their definitions. Think about them. Try to learn them.

Use the new words as soon as you can in conversation or on a school paper. The more you use a word, the better you know it.

You'll never know the meanings of all the words in English (nobody has, does, or ever will know them all), but your vocabulary will grow and grow.

Building up your vocabulary is a lifelong activity. You might be surprised to know that adults look words up all the time, even your English teacher!

There are many words in English that you have to be especially careful about because they're so tricky. And there are lots of words that have the same or opposite meanings. You'll find out about them in the sections on *Homonyms*, *Homographs*, and *Synonyms and Antonyms* later in this chapter.

HOMONYMS/HOMOPHONES

Some people call homonyms *homophones*. Whatever you or your teacher calls them, here's what they are.

> Homonyms are words that are pronounced exactly like other words but have different spellings and different meanings.

Homonyms can play nasty tricks on your spell-checker, so it's important to be able to tell them apart and use them correctly.

See *What About Spell-Checkers?* on page 47.

Here are some of the homonyms that befuddle writers the most. If you're not sure what some of them mean, check your dictionary.

The **heir** to the throne breathed in some fresh **air**.

We are not **allowed** to talk **aloud** in the library.

The construction crew will **alter** the church **altar**.

Last night I **ate** about **eight** of those frosted donuts.

She started to **bawl** when she got hit by the **ball**.

He plays **bass** fiddle in the band and third **base** on the team.

When will that **bee** ever **be** back at this flower?

Little Boy **Blue** said he **blew** his horn.

The **bow** of the ship is made from the **bough** of a tree.

Don't hit the **brake** of your bike too hard or you'll **break** it.

When you walk **by** the store, **buy** some milk. '**Bye** for now.

The state **capitol** building is in the **capital** city of the state.

In each box of the **cereal** was another chapter in the **serial**.

He may **choose** the kind of gum he **chews**.

The lovely **site** on the postcard was a **sight** for sore eyes.

Take a language **course** to improve your **coarse** language.

I'm asking the student **council** to **counsel** me in this matter.

This gold **cymbal** is a **symbol** of the success of our band.

The baby **deer** in the petting zoo was such a **dear** thing.

It takes **dual** weapons to fight a **duel**.

Does a pottery worker **earn** a lot for making an **urn**?

Flee, oh tiny **flea**, before you get squished.

Down the windy **flue** of the chimney **flew** the sickening **flu**.

The farmer raised a clean chicken, not a **foul** that was **fowl**.

The **fourth** marching band in the parade marched **forth**.

The animal covered in **fur** stood under the **fir** tree.

The **gnu** really **knew** the old zoo, not the **new** zoo.

Rabbit fur is sometimes called "**hair** of the **hare**."

The pilot's coat hangs on a **hanger** in the airplane **hangar**.

A foot doctor's job: **He'll** try to **heal** your sore **heel**.

Put your ear **here** and you'll **hear** the mysterious sound.

The cowboy **heard** a thundering **herd** of cattle passing by.

Hie (hurry) up the **high** hill to say **hi** to the climbers.

This sore throat spray is for my **horse** who is **hoarse**.

This quiet **hour** is **our** special time together.

At my island wedding, **I'll** walk down the **aisle** on the **isle**.

The miner **led** me to the **lead** ore in the cave.

To **lessen** the difficulty of the **lesson**, add humor to it.

This is the **lone** bank that will **loan** me money.

The new **maid** has **made** the beds very nicely.

In **Maine** you'll see an animal with a **mane** in the **main** zoo.

That little insect **might** be a **mite** or a tick.

At **night**, the **knight** takes off his shining armor.

No, I do not **know** the answer to every question.

I am **not** very good at tying this complicated **knot**.

Use this **oar** to row to the cave, **or** you won't find the **ore**.

She lifted the heavy **pail**, turned **pale**, and fainted.

A doctor must have **patience** to deal with her **patients**.

If they give up this **piece** of land, there will be **peace**.

When I heard the bell **peal**, I slipped on the banana **peel**.

He works on the **pier** and feels he is everyone's **peer**.

Pray for the animals that other animals **prey** on.

The **principal** instills the **principle** of honesty in students.

Rain fell on the horse's **rein** in the king's **reign**.

I **read** the blue book, the green book, and the **red** book.

Read the directions on how to fit the **reed** on your clarinet.

She will **write** out the **right** words to the ceremonial **rite**.

On my **route** through the woods, I tripped on a tree **root**.

I'll **sail** across the lake to get bargains at the big **sale**.

The **scent** she **sent** me to buy cost more than a **cent**.

From the top of the lighthouse you can **see** miles of **sea**.

The warden of the prison would not **sell** me a jail **cell**.

Sew up the seed bag **so** you can **sow** the seeds.

She rode her **sleigh** into the giant's woods to **slay** him.

The poor bird couldn't **soar** because its wings were **sore**.

Some people think that this **sum** is too high.

Cover your **son** with **sun** block so he won't get a burn.

Walking is good for the **soul**, but the **sole** of my foot hurts.

I'll pound a **stake** into the ground, and you cook us a **steak**.

The **stationery** store doesn't move, so it's **stationary**.

The police arrested them for trying to **steal** the **steel**.

The captain sailed **straight** through the dangerous **strait**.

He wove a fascinating **tale** about the **tail** of the golden lion.

The stadium will **teem** with people to see our **team** play.

They're telling me that **their** car is parked over **there**.

Two people are **too** many **to** sit on one seat.

The weather **vane** fell and cut the **vein** of the **vain** man.

If you stop eating so much, your thick **waist** will **waste** away.

Wait a minute, and I'll tell you the **weight** of your package.

Where do you have to **wear** a tuxedo in a hard**ware** store?

He got sick, and for a **week** he felt very **weak**.

The **weather** will determine **whether** we stay in or go out.

Which broomstick belongs to the **witch**?

He dug a **whole** ton of dirt out of the **hole**.

Who's claiming **whose** kid is smarter?

On the television quiz show, he **won** only **one** dollar.

Thanks for saying that **you're** sorry for **your** mistake.

HOMOGRAPHS

Homographs are words that are spelled exactly alike but have different sounds and different meanings.

Homographs are the opposite of homonyms.

Homonyms: different spellings   same sound

Homographs: same spelling   different sounds

Some people say that homographs can be words that have the same sound but different meanings and origins, but the trickiest homographs are the ones with different sounds. Those are the ones we'll learn about in this section.

The words in parentheses are words that rhyme with or sound like the homographs. They will help you pronounce the homographs correctly. Definitions of the words are in italics.

bass (rhymes with face): *a low-pitched sound*
bass (rhymes with pass): *a type of fish*
The **bass** singer loves to fish for **bass**.

bow (rhymes with no): *a knot with two loops*
bow (rhymes with now): *to bend downward from the waist*
Put this **bow** on your head and take a **bow**.

desert (sounds like duh-**zert**): *to abandon, withdraw from*
desert (sounds like **dez**-ert): *a dry, barren, sandy place*
Never **desert** your post in the hot **desert**.

do (rhymes with goo): *to carry out a task*
do (rhymes with go): *the first note on the scale*
Please **do** sing the scale starting with the note **do**.

does (rhymes with fuzz): *present tense of the verb "to do"*
does (rhymes with foes): *female deer*
Does this zoo have any **does**?

dove (rhymes with love): *a bird associated with peace*
dove (rhymes with stove): *past tense of "to plunge"*
A beautiful **dove dove** out of the sky and swooped down.

drawer (rhymes with sore): *boxlike compartment in a piece of furniture that can be pulled out*
drawer (sounds like draw-er): *a person who draws*
Into the dresser **drawer**, the **drawer** put her drawings.

lead (rhymes with seed): *to show the way*
lead (rhymes with said): *a soft, dense metal*
Will you **lead** me right to the stockpile of **lead**?

Lima (sounds like "**lee**-muh"): *capital city of Peru*
lima (sounds like "I'm a"): *a large, light green bean*
In **Lima** they love to eat **lima** beans for dinner.

live (rhymes with give): *to be alive*
live (rhymes with drive): *having life*
I want to **live** long enough to meet a **live** alien from space.

minute (rhymes with "in it"): *sixty seconds*
minute (rhymes with "my boot"): *exceptionally tiny*
In a **minute** we'll see **minute** atomic particles on the screen.

Polish (pronounced **poh**-lish): *of or relating to Poland*
polish (pronounced **paw**-lish): *liquid used to shine a surface*
The **Polish** company developed a new furniture **polish**.

read (rhymes with reed): *to understand printed words*
read (rhymes with red): *past tense of "to read"*
Read this book and you'll have **read** every book in the library.

row (rhymes with no): *a series of objects in a straight line*
row (rhymes with now): *a big quarrel*
He knocked over her **row** of blocks, and they had a big **row**.

sow (rhymes with no): *to scatter seeds for growing*
sow (rhymes with now): *an adult female hog*
If you **sow** the seeds today, that big **sow** might eat them.

tear (rhymes with chair): *to rip apart*
tear (rhymes with cheer): *a drop of water from an eye*
When she saw him **tear** up her picture, a **tear** came to her eye.

wind (rhymes with find): *to wrap something around*
wind (rhymes with sinned): *air that is moving*
It's impossible to **wind** up the string of this kite in this **wind**.

wound (rhymes with found): *past tense of "to wind"*
wound (rhymes with crooned): *an injury*
The nurse **wound** the bandage tightly around his **wound**.

FIGURES OF SPEECH

Writers who want to be really creative and express themselves in imaginative ways often use figures of speech. These are special ways of using words and phrases to paint vivid word pictures for readers.

People who write poetry use figures of speech a lot, but anyone writing anything can use them to add color and imagination to their words.

Figures of speech are not parts of speech, although you do use parts of speech (nouns, verbs, adjectives, etc.) to create figures of speech. See *Parts of Speech* on page 6.

Alliteration

*Alliteration is pronounced uh-lit-er-**ay**-shun.*

Alliteration is when words close together begin with the same sound (not necessarily the same letter).

A perfect example of alliteration is the old tongue-twister

Peter Piper picked a peck of pickled peppers.

Use alliteration in your writing to

Create a mood: The day dawned damp, dreary, and drab.

Add a bit of humor: Felix Fluster fell flat on his fanny.

Give a character a unique name: George G. Giraffe

Create drama: The hazardous hurricane howls heartlessly through the hollow hills.

Reproduce a sound: Chattering cheerfully, the chipmunks chirped and chuckled.

Label something: Katie's Christmas Candies

> Note that the last example above, *Katie's Christmas Candies*, is an example of alliteration because the three words all begin with the same sound even though the sounds are made with different letters: K, Chi, and C.

Hyperbole

> *Hyperbole* is pronounced *high-**per**-bow-lee*.

Hyperboles are over-the-top exaggerations used for special effect.

Readers don't really believe 100 percent of what they're reading when they see a hyperbole. They know that hyperboles are used to add emphasis and create dramatic, amusing, or remarkable images.

For instance, suppose you read:

> The captain of our basketball team is so tall that he wears a hat with a flashing red light so that helicopters won't bump into his head.

You would know that the writer made up the hat with the red light just to create an exaggerated image of a very tall person.

Use hyperboles in your writing to describe a scene or person in a dramatic, funny, or surprising way that will make the image striking and memorable.

Here are more examples of hyperbole.

We're having a heat wave. The sidewalks are bubbling, the buildings are sweating, and the trees are fanning themselves.

My grandmother could speak about a million languages.

My teacher was so skinny, she came into the classroom through the keyhole in the door.

I have so much homework, I'll be about ninety-nine years old when I finish it.

Similes

Simile is pronounced **sim-i-lee**.

Similes are creative comparisons using the words *like* or *as*. They show imaginative relationships between objects and people that are not alike.

Sometimes, to make an image very vivid, a writer uses an unusual comparison so that the reader will get the picture more sharply.

pretty as a picture	works like a horse
sweet as honey	has cheeks like roses
quiet as a mouse	stings like a bee
stubborn as a mule	sings like a nightingale
slow as molasses	waddles like a duck

CLICHÉS

Overused expressions, like some of those used as examples in this chapter, are called clichés (pronounced: clee-shays). Once they were new and surprising, but with overuse they have become stale. Try to avoid clichés in your writing. If you've seen it many times before, don't use it yourself. Try to think of new ways of expressing your ideas.

Here are some very striking similes.

It's as ridiculous as looking for hot water under the sea.

—old Latin proverb

Baseball games are like snowflakes and fingerprints. No two are ever alike.

—W. P. Kinsella

His hair stood upright like porcupine quills.

—Boccaccio

Happy as a butterfly in a garden full of sunshine and flowers.

— Louisa May Alcott

The mountains were jagged like a page ripped out of a book.

—Kate Grenville

[She] holds a . . . yellow tennis ball up in front of her like the torch on the Statue of Liberty.

—Daphne Merkin

A thunderstorm came rushing down . . . roaring like a brontosaur.

—Carlos Baker

Metaphors

*Metaphor is pronounced **met**-uh-four.*

A metaphor makes a comparison between unlike objects without using the words *like* or *as*.

Similes: My new mattress is as soft *as* a cloud.
My new mattress is *like* a soft cloud.

Metaphor: I sleep on a soft cloud, my new mattress.

A simile tells you that something is *like* another thing.
A metaphor tells you that something *is* another thing.

Here are some metaphors.

She was a moving van, loaded down with all her kids' toys, food, books, clothing, and the kids, too!

I need a new hand cream because my skin is sandpaper.

A good book is a swift ship that sails you on exciting adventures.

He works overtime to pay the mountain of bills he faces.

My math teacher was a human calculator.

Onomatopoeia

*Onomatopoeia is pronounced on-uh-mat-uh-**pee**-uh.*

Onomatopoeia is the use of words that imitate the sounds of sounds.

As you write, you want your readers to experience the full sensations of the scenes you are describing: the sights, smells, tastes, textures, and sounds. Onomatopoeia is the figure of speech that helps you with the sound effects.

See how onomatopoeia helps make the description of the scene below more powerful through the use of sound words.

The burning logs **crackled** in the fireplace as the clock **tick-tocked** its way into the night. Outside, the shutters **whacked** against the side of the house as the wind **howled**, the thunder **rumbled** in the distance, and the trees **creaked**. An old owl **hooted** behind the barn, while back inside the house, the **squeak** of a little mouse aroused the **purring** cat.

Here are some other onomatopoetic words you can use to make

your writing sound more exciting.

clomp	smack	bong	boom
clatter	clack	whiz	bang
crunch	cluck	roar	click
rustle	slurp	hum	ping
splash	quack	ring	sizzle
screech	chirp	honk	squish
squeal	clink	thud	thump
fizz	plop	hiss	pop
clang	buzz	peep	splash

Personification

*Personification is pronounced per-sohn-i-fih-**kay**-shun.*

Personification means giving things that are not alive the qualities of people.

A cloud is not a person. But if writer writes that a "cloud cried tears," instead of "it rained," the writer is personifying the cloud, suggesting that the cloud can weep like a person.

Use personification in your writing to paint vivid word pictures in your readers' minds showing that things can look or act like people.

In the paragraph below, see how the use of personification seems to make the forces of nature come alive by giving them human qualities (the ability to punch, dance, wave, warn, duck, throw things, bark threats, and pour water.)

An unexpected gust of wind came around the corner and punched me in the nose. I dropped my newspaper, which did a swirling dance across the street. The trees waved their arms wildly, warning me to hurry home. The sun suddenly ducked behind the nearest cloud, and the sky threw bolts of lightning to the earth as loud thunder barked its threats at me. Next the heavens poured a tub of water on my head. My poor umbrella surrendered itself to the storm, blew out of my hands, and escaped into the darkness. I tried to do the same.

With personification, you can make a flower smile at a bee, a mountain guard a valley, a penguin wear a tuxedo, and a teakettle whistle a tune.

IDIOMS

Idioms are special expressions and sayings.

These phrases were made up years, even centuries, ago. Experienced readers are usually familiar with most idioms and understand what they mean even though the individual words take on new meanings when used together.

For instance, if someone tells you to "mind your p's and q's," she's asking you to be on your best behavior, to be careful to mind your manners. This expression is at least 400 years old, and word experts think it could have at least three possible origins:

1. The letters *p* and *q* can be confused, so you have to be extra careful about them.
2. In old English pubs people had to pay for the "pints" and "quarts" they drank.
3. "Pieds" and "queues" are dance steps that French dancers had to perform carefully.

Today it doesn't really matter how an idiom originated as long as you know what it means.

Use an idiom in your writing when it perfectly fits what you're trying to express, but be careful not to overdo it. Most idioms are so familiar that they're clichés, and you want your writing to be fresh and original.

See *Clichés* on page 143.

There are thousands of idioms in the English language. Here is a sampling of some of the best known from A to Z.

Ants in your pants
very restless, can't sit still

Barking up the wrong tree
having the wrong idea about something

Cat got your tongue?
Why don't you speak?

Don't count your chickens before they hatch.
Don't be too sure that things are going to work out the way you think they will until they do.

Every cloud has a silver lining.
In every bad situation there is something good.

Feather in your cap
an honor or accomplishment to be proud of

Get up on the wrong side of the bed
to wake up in a grumpy, grouchy mood

Hard nut to crack
a very difficult problem to solve

In hot water
in a lot of trouble

Jump down someone's throat
to scream or yell at someone angrily

Keep your shirt on.
Stay calm; don't get angry; be patient.

Lay an egg
to fail totally at something; give an embarrassing performance

Make a mountain out of a molehill
to make a small issue into an important one by exaggerating it

Out of the woods
safe from danger or trouble

The pen is mightier than the sword.
Writing about something accomplishes more than fighting about it.

Quick on the draw
mentally alert; quick to learn new things; fast to respond

Red tape
rules and regulations that waste a lot of time

Security blanket
something that you hold on to that makes you feel more secure or safe

Tickled pink
very happy, amused, delighted, or pleased

Upset the applecart
to spoil a plan suddenly or accidentally

Wet behind the ears
inexperienced, new to the job; young, immature

X marks the spot.
This is the exact place we are looking for.

You can't teach an old dog new tricks.
Some people are set in their ways and don't want to try new ways of doing things.

Zip it up!
Be quiet. Stop talking.

SYNONYMS AND ANTONYMS

Synonyms are words that have the same meaning.

Because there are so many words in the English language, there are often many different words you can choose that will express your thoughts perfectly.

For instance, you could write that the monster was *big*. But to make your sentence more dramatic and emphatic, you could write that he was *huge*, *immense*, *gigantic*, *enormous*, *mammoth*, *tremendous*, *titanic*, *colossal*, *massive*, or *gargantuan*. Wow!

All those words are synonyms of *big*. The *s* in *synonym* should remind you of *same* meaning.

The opposite of *synonym* is *antonym*.

An antonym is a word with the opposite meaning.

Suppose, in your story, a small person, the very opposite of the giant, was going to fight the big guy. You could describe this person as *small*, of course, or you could use one of the many other antonyms of *big* to emphasize how opposite your two characters are: *tiny*, *little*, *diminutive*, *miniature*, *minute*, *infinitesimal*, *minuscule*, *microscopic*, *teensy-weensy*, *itty-bitty*, and *Lilliputian*. Wow again!

Where do you find all these synonyms and antonyms? In a special book called a *thesaurus*. A thesaurus is a listing of thousands of words and their synonyms and antonyms. No writer should ever be without a good thesaurus. Many word processing programs have thesauruses built in. Learn how to use yours so you can add new, colorful, expressive words to your writing.

Here are some examples of synonyms and antonyms for just the common, everyday word *good* that you can find in a typical thesaurus.

In your thesaurus or dictionary, **syn** means synonyms and **ant** means antonyms.

good

syn	*ant*
acceptable	deficient
adequate	deleterious
advantageous	detrimental
all right	disagreeable
appropriate	displeasing
benefic	dissatisfactory
beneficial	ill-behaved
brave	improper
convenient	inadequate
favorable	inauspicious
favoring	inferior
fit	injurious
helpful	misbehaving
moral	unpleasant
nice	decayed
proper	poor
propitious	putrid
satisfactory	rotten

syn	*ant*
sufficient	rotten
suitable	spoiled
tolerable	unacceptable
upright	unsatisfactory
useful	unfavorable
virtuous	wrong

How to Use This Thesaurus

MAIN ENTRY WORDS

Synonyms are grouped together after main entry words. These main entries are listed alphabetically and printed in yellow type. Suppose you need a synonym for *exaggerate*. This thesaurus has a main entry for *exaggerate* with nine synonyms:

> exaggerate *vb* overstate, overdo, inflate, embellish, embroider, elaborate, gild, magnify, dramatize

If a main entry word has more than one sense or use, the synonyms are grouped in numbered senses, as in the entry for *boast*, which can either be a verb or a noun:

> boast 1. *vb* brag, gloat, crow, show off, vaunt, swagger, exult
> 2. *n* brag, bragging, vaunt, claim, assertion, bluster, swagger, bravado

PART-OF-SPEECH LABELS

Each entry or numbered sense has a part-of-speech label that identifies the part of speech of the main entry and the synonyms of each sense. The part-of-speech labels are:

n	noun	*prep*	preposition
vb	verb	*conj*	conjunction
adj	adjective	*interj*	interjection
adv	adverb	*pron*	pronoun

ANTONYMS

Antonyms are words that mean the opposite of other words. Sometimes you can find a clearer way to express your idea by putting it in opposite terms. Some synonyms are followed by antonyms printed inside parentheses:

> afraid *adj* scared, frightened, alarmed, terrified, petrified, aghast, scared, timorous (antonym: brave)

able 1. *adj* capable, competent, qualified, eligible, authorized, suitable, fit

2. *adj* accomplished, proficient, skillful, adept, clever, handy, dexterous, deft, smart, expert, practical

abolish *vb* end, eradicate, exterminate, eliminate, revoke, cancel, obliterate, repeal, rescind, annul, nullify, countermand, disallow, veto, overrule, finish, destroy, erase ANTONYM: *save*

about 1. *adv* approximately, around, roughly, nearly, almost, practically

2. *adv* around, round, all around, everywhere, nearby

3. *prep* concerning, regarding, touching, relating to

4. *prep* around, near, at

absent *adj* away, missing, elsewhere, astray, AWOL, lost ANTONYM: *present*

abuse 1. *vb* misuse, mistreat, torment, oppress, suppress, repress, ill-treat, maltreat, torture, persecute, victimize, molest, harass, hurt, insult, punish

2. *n* misuse, mistreatment, ill-treatment, injury, harm, punishment, torture

accent 1. *n* stress, emphasis, prominence, beat, cadence, diacritic

2. *n* pronunciation, inflection, drawl, twang, burr, dialect

3. *n* decoration

4. *vb* emphasize

accident 1. *n* mishap, setback, collision, disaster, emergency

2. *n* chance

accidentally *adv* unintentionally, inadvertently, unwittingly, unconsciously, fortuitously, incidentally ANTONYM: *purposely*

accuracy *n* exactness, precision, correctness, exactitude, truth

act 1. *vb* perform, work, function, operate, execute, stage, carry out, ply, serve, go, do

2. *vb* behave, seem, appear

3. *vb* perform, play, enact, stage, portray, dramatize, impersonate, pose, render, pretend

4. *n* deed, action, feat, accomplishment, achievement, exploit,

undertaking, step, work

5. *n* bill, law, decree, statute, ordinance, legislation, rule

6. *n* performance, routine, number, sketch, bit, skit, pretense

active *adj* animated, spirited, dynamic, busy, vibrant, bustling, frenetic, hyperactive, strenuous, athletic, lively, alive ANTONYM: *passive*

add 1. *vb* sum, total, calculate, compute, tally, count, score ANTONYM: *subtract*

2. *vb* combine, include, append, annex, supplement, incorporate, integrate, join

adjacent 1. *adj* adjoining, neighboring, bordering, abutting, tangent, next, next door, near

2. *prep* beside

adjust *vb* alter, modify, regulate, adapt, tailor, accommodate, conform, acclimatize, orient, change, fix, arrange

adopt 1. *vb* embrace, appropriate, assume, espouse, approve, choose, use

2. *vb* foster, take in, raise, rear

advantage *n* benefit, profit, superiority, convenience, vantage, upper hand, asset, virtue, plus, avail

advertise *vb* publicize, announce, promote, proclaim, declare, broadcast, pitch, parade, flaunt, plug, tell, show

advice *n* guidance, counsel, recommendation, suggestion, caution, admonition, tip, warning

affect 1. *vb* influence, impress, move, sway

2. *vb* act, pretend

3. *n* emotion

afraid *adj* scared, frightened, alarmed, terrified, petrified, aghast, scared, timorous, anxious, nervous, cowardly ANTONYM: *brave*

again *adv* once more, anew, afresh, over, encore

agent 1. *n* representative, intermediary, middleman, broker, executor, liaison, delegate, spokesperson, go-between, handler, seller

2. *n* spy

agree 1. *vb* consent, assent, concur, accept, accede ANTONYM: *argue, object*

2. *vb* match, correspond, coincide, harmonize, accord, jibe, suit

air 1. *n* sky, heaven, atmosphere, stratosphere, troposphere, space

2. *n* breath, ventilation, oxygen wind

3. *n* quality, appearance

4. *vb* broadcast, play, say

alike 1. *adj* similar, like, analogous, comparable, equivalent, parallel, close, akin, same ANTONYM: *different*

2. *adv* similarly, likewise, comparably, analogously

alive *adj* living, live, animate, animated, vital, viable, quick, organic, lively, active ANTONYM: *dead*

all 1. *n, pron* everything, everyone, everybody, sum, whole, totality, total

2. *adj* every, entire, each, complete, whole, total

3. *adv* completely

alone *adj* lone, solitary, isolated, unaccompanied, unattended, solo, single-handed, lonely, single

alternate 1. *vb* reciprocate, oscillate, fluctuate, switch

2. *adj* alternating, every other, periodic

3. *n* substitute, replacement, backup, surrogate, double

ancestor *n* forebear, forefather, progenitor, forerunner, predecessor,

antecedent, patriarch, matriarch, elder, parent

angel *n* spirit, sprite, archangel, seraph, cherub

angry *adj* mad, furious, upset, annoyed, irritated, aggravated, exasperated, indignant, irate, infuriated, livid, bitter, sore, cross, belligerent, violent

animal 1. *n* creature, beast, brute, being, organism, monster
2. *adj* bestial, beastly, brutish

announcement *n* declaration, notice, notification, proclamation, report, statement, pronouncement, news, revelation, bulletin, message, tidings, advertisement

answer 1. *n* reply, response, retort, rejoinder, riposte, reaction, reciprocation ANTONYM: *question*
2. *n* solution, key, result, explanation, resolution, product ANTONYM: *problem, question*
3. *vb* reply, respond, retort, acknowledge, echo, counter, react, reciprocate ANTONYM: *question*
4. *vb* solve
5. *vb* satisfy

anticipate 1. *vb* foresee, expect, look forward to, predict
2. *vb* hope

anxious 1. *adj* worried, apprehensive, uneasy, disturbed, insecure, afraid, nervous, tense
2. *adj* eager

anyway *adv* anyhow, nevertheless, nonetheless, however, regardless, notwithstanding, still

apology *n* excuse, acknowledgment, regrets, explanation

apparently 1. *adv* evidently, seemingly, presumably, supposedly, reputedly, probably

2. *adv* clearly, obviously, plainly, patently

appear 1. *vb* emerge, arise, rise, surface, materialize, come into view, show up, turn up, form, come

2. *vb* act

3. *vb* look

appointment 1. *n* selection, nomination, election, designation, assignment, delegation, installation, investiture, ordination choice

2. *n* meeting, visit

3. *n* profession

appreciate 1. *vb* value, prize, cherish, treasure, relish, savor, respect

2. *vb* thank, enjoy, welcome

3. *vb* understand

approach 1. *vb* come near, draw near, near, advance, loom, gravitate toward, come

2. *vb* address, accost, speak to, talk ANTONYM: *avoid*

3. *n* coming, arrival, appearance, advent, entry

4. *n* method, treatment

approve 1. *vb* endorse, support, authorize, sanction, certify, ratify, validate, legalize, affirm, agree, back

2. *vb* accept, favor, applaud, recommend, acclaim, commend, appreciate

approximate 1. *adj* rough, inexact, estimated, close, near, ballpark, general

2. *vb* estimate

3. *vb* resemble

argue 1. *vb* quarrel, debate, dispute, disagree, bicker, squabble, quibble, wrangle, fight ANTONYM: *agree*

2. *vb* claim, maintain, plead, assert, contend, allege, charge, protest

aristocracy *n* nobility, gentry, elite, upper class, society, high society, haut monde *(French)*, jet set, rich

arrange 1. *vb* organize, sort, classify, order, file, systematize, categorize, determine, array, structure, place, rank, orient, orientate, adjust, straighten

2. *vb* plan, devise, set up, schedule

art *n* skill, craft, technique, artistry, craftsmanship, creativity, artifice, talent

ask *vb* inquire, request, question, interrogate, query, quiz, examine, interview, grill, petition, apply, beg

assortment *n* variety, mix, selection, collection, compilation, array, miscellany, range, series, gamut, medley, potpourri, hash, pile, mess

assume 1. *vb* presume, postulate, presuppose, surmise, gather, guess, believe, pretend

2. *vb* adopt, bear

attack 1. *vb* invade, assault, charge, ambush, waylay, mug, storm, raid, besiege, harry, assail, ravage, bombard, strike, fight, argue, pillage ANTONYM: *protect*

2. *n* assault, raid, invasion, charge, offensive, offense, incursion, strike, sally, sortie, foray, onset, onslaught, counterattack, operation, sack

3. *n* fit

attention 1. *n* concentration, awareness, alertness, thought, consideration, diligence

2. *n* notice

attractive *adj* appealing, fascinating, captivating, magnetic, alluring, inviting, desirable, intriguing, charming, charismatic, winning, pretty, pleasant

audience *n* spectators, viewers, onlookers, readers, listeners, patrons, congregation, gallery, meeting, patron

automatic 1. *adj* automated, mechanical, mechanized, motorized, self-starting, self-acting, computerized

2. *adj* habitual, involuntary, instinctive, mechanical, spontaneous, reflex, unintentional

available *adj* accessible, usable, convenient, handy, ready

average 1. *adj* unexceptional, mediocre, unremarkable, standard, routine, medium, modest, common, normal

2. *n* mean, median, midpoint, standard, medium, par, norm

avoid *vb* shun, dodge, evade, shirk, duck, sidestep, elude, avert, bypass, circumvent, escape

awesome 1. *adj* amazing, impressive, astonishing, miraculous, terrific, sensational, grand, great

2. *adj* scary

awful *adj* terrible, horrible, dreadful, dire, ghastly, appalling, wretched, grievous, disagreeable, atrocious, outrageous, disgraceful, hateful, odious, bad, gruesome

axis *n* pivot, fulcrum, swivel, hinge, middle

bad 1. *adj* evil, sinful, naughty, infamous, villainous, nefarious, incorrigible, disreputable, wicked, improper, mischievous, dishonest, immoral ANTONYM: *good*

2. *adj* unpleasant, disagreeable, undesirable, objectionable, miserable, lousy, nasty, offensive, abominable, repulsive, detestable, despicable, vile, nauseating, sickening, unsavory, disgusting, obnoxious, distasteful, awful

3. *adj* rotten, spoiled, rancid, decayed, putrid, moldy, stale

4. *adj* sad

5. *adj* unhealthy

6. *adj* wrong

bag 1. *n* sack, pouch, purse, handbag, pocketbook, satchel, tote bag, tote, backpack, pack, knapsack, fanny pack, container, luggage, wallet

2. *n* base

3. *vb* catch

balance 1. *n* stability, equilibrium, footing, poise

2. *n* symmetry, harmony, counterbalance, proportion, equilibrium

3. *n* remainder

4. *vb* stabilize, counterbalance, steady, poise, counterpoise, neutralize, equalize, redeem, compensate, coordinate, offset

band 1. *n* group

2. *n* group, orchestra, ensemble, combo

3. *n* stripe, ribbon, belt, girdle, sash, tape, border, strip, streak, seam, vein row, zone, ring

bang 1. *n* crash, crack, pop, boom, blast, explosion, report, thud, detonation, clang, rumble, clap, thunder, noise, knock

2. *vb* rattle, clatter, clash, clank, bump, knock, hit, collide

barrier *n* obstacle, obstruction, hindrance, hurdle, difficulty, impediment, barricade, roadblock, blockade, palisade, clog, divider

base 1. *n* foundation, bottom, support, footing, foot, root, floor
ANTONYM: *top*

2. *n* basis

3. *n* headquarters, home, home base, base camp, camp, station, terminal

4. *n* plate, goal, bag, sack

5. *vb* found, ground, predicate, establish

6. *vb* locate, station, post, situate

basic *adj* elemental, elementary, fundamental, staple, rudimentary, primitive, introductory, primary, necessary

basis *n* foundation, support, justification, grounds, authority, underpinning, raison d'être, cornerstone, rudiment, base, cause

bear 1. *vb* endure, stand, tolerate, abide, stomach, suffer, accept, brook, take, shoulder, assume, undertake, experience

2. *vb* carry

3. *vb* support, afford

4. *vb* give

beautiful *adj* gorgeous, glamorous, exquisite, beauteous, elegant, stunning, ravishing, dazzling, magnificent, pretty ANTONYM: *ugly*

because *conj* since, due to, for, as, on account of

before 1. *adv* previously, formerly, earlier, already, beforehand, yet

2. *prep* prior to, ahead of, preceding, until

beginning *n* origin, source, outset, onset, commencement, initiation, inauguration, start, birth, conception, genesis, infancy, threshold, front ANTONYM: *finish, conclusion*

behavior 1. *n* conduct, manners, etiquette, decorum, bearing

2. *n* performance, function, operation, execution

belief 1. *n* conviction, opinion, view, notion, mind, instinct, hunch, suspicion, attitude, sentiment, theory, idea, feeling, perspective

2. *n* faith, trust, confidence, credit, credence, understanding, certainty

3. *n* creed, doctrine, dogma, credo, principle, religion, philosophy, superstition

believe 1. *vb* accept, think, hold, deem, trust, acknowledge, affirm, view ANTONYM: *deny*

2. *vb* guess

belong *vb* fit, go, fit in, pertain, apply, relate, concern

bend 1. *vb* twist, curve, wind, arch, warp, flex, buckle, bow, droop, veer, meander, thread, contort, distort, turn, slant ANTONYM: *straighten*

2. *vb* bow, curtsy, genuflect, stoop, kneel, crouch, squat, duck, hunch, slouch, slump

3. *n* twist, kink, crimp, curl, tangle, curve, corner

beside *prep* next to, alongside, adjoining, adjacent to, against, near, with

best 1. *adj* finest, choicest, first, prime, premium, optimum, preeminent, leading, unparalleled, unsurpassed, superlative, foremost, ultimate, supreme, prime, top, upper, good ANTONYM: *worst*

2. *adv* most, above all ANTONYM: *least*

3. *vb* defeat, exceed

better 1. *adj* finer, greater, preferable, improved, superior, good, best

2. *adj* improved, improving, convalescent, convalescing, healthy

3. *adv* more

4. *vb* exceed

5. *vb* defeat

between *prep* among, amid, amongst, amidst, betwixt, through

big *adj* large, generous, substantial, considerable, giant, stout, stocky, great, huge, heavy, fat, infinite, abundant, high ANTONYM: *small*

bit 1. *n* piece, fragment, particle, scrap, shred, chip, flake, fleck, trifle, snippet, snatch, bite, block, part

2. *n* trace, hint, suggestion, shade, touch, lick, glimmer, dash, pinch, tang, modicum, jot, iota, shred

3. *n* role, act

bite 1. *vb* chew, gnaw, nibble, munch, taste, chomp, nip, snap

2. *n* morsel, taste, mouthful, nibble, scrap, bit, meal

black *adj, n* ebony, jet, sable, raven, inky, pitch-black, coal-black, dark ANTONYM: *white*

blame 1. *vb* censure, criticize, condemn, denounce, accuse, implicate, charge, try, scold ANTONYM: *forgive*

2. *n* guilt

blank 1. *adj* empty, clean

2. *adj* expressionless, vacuous, impassive, vacant, deadpan, poker-faced

bleak *adj* dreary, desolate, somber, grim, depressing, drear, hopeless, cheerless, gloomy, oppressive, dismal, dour, sad, sterile, pessimistic

block 1. *n* piece, chunk, cube, cake, slice, slab, bar, hunk, wedge, bit, part

2. *n* neighborhood, building

3. *vb* hide

4. *vb* bar

blush *vb* flush, redden, color, glow

boast 1. *vb* brag, gloat, crow, show off, vaunt, swagger, exult

2. *n* brag, bragging, vaunt, claim, assertion, bluster, swagger, bravado

body 1. *n* build, physique, frame, anatomy, figure, form, torso, trunk

2. *n* corpse, carcass, cadaver, remains, skeleton, bones

3. *n* human being

4. *n* group

5. *n* matter

6. *n* density

book *n* volume, publication, text, paperback, hardcover, work, tome, manual, handbook, audiobook, manuscript, script, libretto, pamphlet

border 1. *n* frontier, boundary, march, borderland, edge, circumference, band

2. *vb* abut, adjoin, neighbor, bound, skirt, flank, join

bored *adj* uninterested, jaded, blasé, tired

boss 1. *n* chief, leader, head, director, employer, foreman, manager, supervisor, superior, captain, commander, skipper, principal, chairperson

2. *vb* lead, control

bother 1. *vb* annoy, vex, tease, plague, pester, needle, aggravate, irk, nag, hound, badger, harass, bug, irritate, chafe, rankle, disturb, worry

2. *n* nuisance

brave 1. *adj* courageous, heroic, fearless, valiant, valorous, gallant, bold, stalwart, daring, audacious, intrepid, dauntless, undaunted, adventurous, adventuresome, plucky, dashing ANTONYM: *afraid*

2. *vb* face

break 1. *vb* crack, shatter, smash, fracture, split, snap, crash, splinter, burst, rupture, crush, squash, chip, destroy, explode, separate

2. *n* fracture, split, crack, rift, breach, gap, opening, chip, schism

3. *n* pause, recess, intermission, breather, respite, delay, interlude, interruption, lull, hiatus, suspension, disruption vacation, rest, truce

4. *vb* disobey

5. *vb* defeat

6. *n* luck

breathe 1. *vb* inhale, exhale, respire, expire, pant, gasp, wheeze, puff, huff, gulp, mumble

2. *vb* live

bridge 1. *n* span, overpass, catwalk, gangway, gangplank, viaduct

2. *n* link

3. *vb* cross, connect, span, join

bright 1. *adj* brilliant, glowing, radiant, sunny, dazzling, glaring, blazing, intense, luminous, colorful, gay, vivid, flashy, fair, shiny ANTONYM: *dim, dull*

2. *adj* happy

3. *adj* smart

bring *vb* fetch, deliver, lead, conduct, escort, take, lead, carry, pull

broken 1. *adj* cracked, shattered, fractured, damaged, defective, faulty, malfunctioning, disabled, broken-down, down, unusable, out of order, useless

2. *adj* tame

brush 1. *n* underbrush, undergrowth, shrubbery, scrub, thicket, bushes, hedge

2. *n* meeting

3. *vb* clean, sweep, rub

4. *vb* comb

build 1. *vb* construct, erect, assemble, raise, fabricate, fashion form, invent, make ANTONYM: *destroy*

2. *vb* strengthen

3. *n* body

burn 1. *vb* blaze, flare, incinerate, scorch, singe, sear, char, glow, smoke, cook

2. *vb* hurt

business 1. *n* industry, commerce, trade, traffic, manufacturing, finance, economics

2. *n* affair, matter, concern, transaction, job

3. *n* company, firm, establishment, corporation, enterprise, outfit, partnership, concern, factory

but 1. *conj* however, although, though, yet, except, nevertheless
2. *prep* except, besides, save, excluding, barring

buy 1. *vb* purchase, pay for, barter, shop, get, hire
2. *n* bargain

call 1. *vb* summon, beckon, invite, page, accost, welcome, visit
2. *vb, n* yell
3. *vb* phone, telephone, ring, dial, buzz
4. *vb* name
5. *n* attraction
6. *n* reason

calm 1. *adj* peaceful, serene, tranquil, placid, undisturbed, untroubled, composed, self-possessed, relaxed, poised, quiet, gentle
2. *n* quiet, tranquility, peacefulness, serenity, stillness, composure, silence, hush, peace ANTONYM: *activity*
3. *vb* quiet, relax, soothe, ease, comfort, compose, lull, pacify ANTONYM: *excite*

candidate *n* nominee, aspirant, applicant, office-seeker, front-runner, dark horse, favorite son, contestant

careful 1. *adj* painstaking, thorough, exact, accurate, particular, precise, meticulous, conscientious, studious, scrupulous, nice
2. *adj* cautious, wary, prudent, concerned, circumspect, politic, discreet, judicious, guarded, alert, suspicious ANTONYM: *thoughtless*

carry 1. *vb* move, transport, convey, bear, cart, pack, haul, transfer, tote, take
2. *vb* sell
3. *vb* support

castle *n* fortress, fort, garrison, fortification, stronghold, citadel, keep, donjon, palace

catch 1. *vb* capture, trap, grasp, take, bag, snag, clasp, snare, ensnare, entangle, mire, enslave, seize, arrest ANTONYM: *free*

2. *vb* pass, overtake, outrun, outstrip

3. *vb* contract, develop, come down with, incur, get

4. *n* grab, snag, scoop

5. *n* clasp, lock

6. *n* trap

cause 1. *vb* produce, create, effect, generate, prompt, inspire, motivate, engender, start, make, do

2. *n* origin, source, stimulus, basis, reason

3. *n* principle, conviction, movement

celebrate 1. *vb* observe, commemorate, keep, solemnize, honor, praise

2. *vb* rejoice, carouse, revel, party

ceremony 1. *n* service, ritual, rite, celebration, tradition, commemoration, festival

2. *n* formality, pomp, solemnity, protocol

certain 1. *adj* sure, positive, confident, definite, assertive, forceful, vehement, self-confident, assured, convinced

2. *adj* undeniable, unquestionable, definite, absolute, inevitable, inescapable, unavoidable, reliable, conclusive, infallible

3. *adj* special

4. *adj* reliable

chance 1. *n* fate, fortune, luck, destiny, lot, accident, coincidence, happenstance, serendipity

2. *n* possibility

3. *n* opportunity

4. *adj* arbitrary, accidental

5. *vb* happen

change 1. *vb* alter, vary, modify, transform, convert, mutate, shift, innovate, correct, adjust, distort, tinker

2. *vb* switch, exchange, replace, interchange, substitute, swap, reverse, invert, transpose, trade

3. *n* alteration, variation, shift, deviation, evolution, mutation, transformation, revolution, modification, metamorphosis, transition, vicissitude

channel *n* trough, chute, gutter, sluice, shaft, ramp, slide, groove, furrow, trench, rut, ditch, moat, aqueduct, canal, waterway, artery, pipe, course

cheap 1. *adj* inexpensive, reasonable, affordable, economical, low-priced, cut-rate, budget ANTONYM: *expensive*

2. *adj* inferior, shoddy, mediocre, second-rate, chintzy

3. *adj* thrifty, frugal, prudent, stingy, miserly, niggardly, tight-fisted, penny-pinching, cheeseparing, penurious, tight

cheat 1. *vb* trick, deceive, swindle, chisel, hoodwink, beguile, bluff, defraud, dupe, con, gyp, prey on, fool

2. *n* cheater, swindler, quack, charlatan, fraud, shyster, imposter, fake, humbug, criminal, hypocrite

childish *adj* childlike, infantile, immature, juvenile, puerile, sophomoric, young

choice 1. *n* alternative, option, selection, pick, preference, way, recourse, vote, voice, preference

2. *adj* good, favorite, special

choose *vb* select, pick, elect, opt, name, take, designate, vote, decide, prefer ANTONYM: *exclude*

circle 1. *n* ring, loop, hoop, disk, coil, circuit, circumference, perimeter, periphery, revolution, orbit, round
2. *vb* ring

citizen *n* inhabitant, subject, native, resident, national, denizen, occupant

civilization 1. *n* cultivation, culture, enlightenment, refinement, breeding, polish, progress
2. *n* people

clarity *n* clearness, lucidity, simplicity, transparency, definition, focus, sharpness, resolution

clean 1. *vb* wash, cleanse, rinse, scrub, scrape, scour, launder, bathe, brush, tidy, purify, sterilize, filter, shine, sweep
2. *adj* spotless, washed, unblemished, unused, unsoiled, fresh, blank, pristine, immaculate, neat, sterile ANTONYM: *dirty*

climb 1. *vb* scale, clamber, scramble, crawl, ascend
2. *n* ascent, ascension, rise, growth, slant

clothes *n* clothing, dress, apparel, wardrobe, garments, attire, garb, vestments, finery, habit

cold *adj* frosty, icy, freezing, frigid, arctic, polar, antarctic, raw, cool ANTONYM: *hot*

collide *vb* crash, smash, impact, sideswipe, rear-end, hit, knock

colony 1. *n* possession, dependency, settlement, satellite, state, country
2. *n* herd

come *vb* arrive, reach, appear, attain, approach, descend ANTONYM: *go*

comfortable 1. *adj* cozy, snug, comfy, restful, homey, roomy, spacious ANTONYM: *uncomfortable*
2. *adj* rich

committee *n* board, council, panel, commission, subcommittee, delegation, mission, cabinet, assembly

common 1. *adj* ordinary, typical, familiar, everyday, widespread, average, unpretentious, humble, commonplace, pedestrian, popular, prevalent, general, normal, usual, plain ANTONYM: *strange*

2. *adj* vulgar, coarse, commonplace, crass, crude, banal, plebeian, cheap, dirty

3. *adj* communal, mutual, joint, collective, collaborative, shared, unanimous, public

4. *n* park

compare *vb* contrast, juxtapose, parallel, liken, match, correlate, study, distinguish

compete *vb* contend, rival, play, contest, vie, fight, face

complain *vb* protest, gripe, grouch, grumble, whine, nag, fuss, moan, groan, mumble, object

complete 1. *adj* entire, full, total, whole, absolute, utter, uncut, intact, unbroken, exhaustive, thorough, unabridged, uncensored, all, comprehensive, perfect

2. *vb* finish

concentrate 1. *vb* focus, devote, attend, meditate, think, study

2. *vb* focus, converge, consolidate, condense, compress, intensify, thicken, distill, gather

conclusion 1. *n* inference, assumption, deduction decision ANTONYM: *beginning*

2. *n* afterword, epilogue, postscript, postlude, coda ANTONYM: *introduction*

3. *n* finish

confuse *vb* perplex, puzzle, bewilder, confound, complicate, baffle, disconcert, disorient, befuddle, abash, stymie, mystify, throw, stump

conservative *adj* conventional, traditional, orthodox, moderate, reactionary, right-wing, illiberal, stuffy ANTONYM: *liberal*

consider *vb* reflect, weigh, entertain, contemplate, study, think

contain 1. *vb* hold, include, consist of, comprise, accommodate, carry, embody
2. *vb* restrain, limit, suppress, curb, quell, quash, quench, control, repress, swallow, stop, extinguish, prevent

continue 1. *vb* last, endure, remain, persist, persevere, carry on, proceed
2. *vb* resume, recommence, renew, pick up, start

contradict *vb* deny, refute, challenge, dispute, object, discredit

control 1. *vb* command, direct, manage, dominate, subject, regulate, engineer, tame, captain, cope, handle, harness, govern, lead, contain
2. *vb* contain
3. *n* rule, discipline

cool 1. *adj* chilly, chill, brisk, fresh, bracing, nippy, cold
2. *adj* remote, aloof, distant, reserved, chilly, impersonal, calm, apathetic, unfriendly
3. *adj* excellent, all right, fashionable, good
4. *vb* chill, refrigerate, freeze, congeal, fan

copy 1. *n* reproduction, facsimile, photocopy, likeness, duplicate
2. *vb* reproduce, imitate

correct 1. *adj* accurate, right, exact, precise, true, faultless, flawless, authentic, faithful, factual, perfect ANTONYM: *wrong*
2. *adj* respectable, decent, proper, fitting, appropriate, seemly, decorous, becoming, fit, prim

3. *vb* remedy, rectify, revise, edit, amend, emend, reconcile, improve, reform, redress, fix, adjust, perfect, change

4. *vb* punish

country 1. *n* nation, republic, kingdom, dominion, realm, commonwealth, land, domain, homeland, fatherland, motherland, state, colony

2. *n* countryside, landscape, hinterland, wilderness, wild, backwoods, frontier, bush

3. *n* music

courage *n* bravery, valor, fortitude, boldness, spirit, gallantry, heroism, daring, audacity, nerve, mettle, grit, stomach

course 1. *n* path, route, direction, heading, bearing, way, itinerary

2. *n* track, racetrack, trail, road

3. *n* class, subject, seminar, program, major, minor, colloquium, elective

court 1. *n* courtyard, square, quadrangle, quad, atrium, patio, plaza, piazza, cloister

2. *n* field

3. *n* tribunal, law court, bench, bar, judiciary, forum

4. *n* courthouse, courtroom

5. *n* retinue, entourage, cortege, royal household, attendants

6. *vb* woo, date, romance, flirt, love

cover 1. *vb* cover up, blanket, carpet, spread, coat, overspread, surface, pave, flag, wrap, protect, plate

2. *vb* hide

3. *n* top

4. *n* blanket, wrapper

5. *n* protection

crime *n* offense, violation, sin, evil, wrong, wrongdoing, misdeed, trespass, transgression, infraction, felony, misdemeanor, theft, treason, murder

crowd *n* mob, multitude, host, throng, army, legion, horde, swarm, flock, band, group, troop

cry 1. *vb* weep, sob, wail, bawl, whimper, whine, moan, groan

2. *n, vb* shout, scream, howl, screech, bellow, shriek, roar, whoop, squeal, bay, yowl, wail, squawk, noise, yell, bark

curious 1. *adj* inquisitive, prying, nosy, inquiring, meddlesome

2. *adj* strange

cut 1. *vb* chop, slice, dice, mince, shred, grate, carve, cleave, gouge, hew, hack, lacerate, amputate, rip, peel, carve

2. *vb* trim, shave, clip, snip, shear, prune, mow, reap

3. *vb* condense, decrease

4. *n* gash, slash, wound, injury, incision, laceration, scrape, scratch, nick, gouge, cleft, notch, slit, rip, hole, sore

cute *adj* adorable, charming, quaint, cutesy, pretty

damage 1. *n* destruction, wreckage, wear, devastation, desolation, ruin, havoc, mayhem, injury, sabotage, decay, harm

2. *vb* impair, mar, deface, scratch, scrape, scar, disfigure, deform, distort, hurt, break, destroy

dangerous *adj* harmful, perilous, hazardous, unsafe, risky, treacherous, precarious, explosive, deadly, destructive ANTONYM: *safe*

dark 1. *adj* gloomy, murky, dusky, shady, unlit, somber, overcast, pitch-black, black, opaque, dim

2. *adj* brunette, brown, tan, black, swarthy, sable, ebony

3. *n* darkness, dusk, gloom, blackness, shade, shadow, night

dead 1. *adj* deceased, departed, late, lifeless, extinct, defunct, inanimate ANTONYM: *alive*

2. *adj* inert, still, stagnant, motionless, calm

3. *adj* tired

4. *adv* completely

5. *n* casualty

decay 1. *vb* deteriorate, disintegrate, crumble, decompose, wear, rot, molder, spoil, putrefy, corrode, destroy

2. *n* deterioration, degeneration, decomposition, spoilage, disrepair, disintegration, corrosion damage

decide *vb* settle, resolve, determine, rule, conclude, reconcile, negotiate, mediate, arbitrate, judge, adjudge, convict, choose

decorate 1. *vb* adorn, beautify, ornament, embellish, trim, garnish, bedeck, redecorate, refurbish, festoon

2. *vb* praise

decrease 1. *vb* lessen, diminish, abate, decline, wane, subside, ebb, dwindle, taper, shrink, shrivel, reduce, depress, lower, slash, curtail, cut, condense, weaken, shrink

2. *n* drop

defeat 1. *vb* conquer, beat, overcome, surmount, overpower, vanquish, best, better, top, break, overthrow, throw, upset, down, whip, crush, subdue, win

2. *n* loss, downfall, failure, conquest, destruction, rout, upset, beating, thrashing ANTONYM: *victory*

delay 1. *vb* postpone, defer, put off, deter, stall, procrastinate, wait, hesitate

2. *vb* hamper, detain, impede, hinder, retard, prevent

3. *n* break

department *n* section, division, branch, bureau, agency, chapter, subsidiary, affiliate, field, business, job, arm

departure 1. *n* exit, going, leaving, withdrawal, farewell, embarkation, exodus, escape

2. *n* deviation, divergence, digression, aberration, irregularity, change, difference

depend 1. *vb* trust, rely, count on, believe

2. *vb* hang, hinge, rest, turn

depression 1. *n* dent

2. *n* desolation, despair, despondency, dejection, sorrow, misery

3. *n* recession, slump, decline, downturn, crash

describe *vb* characterize, define, depict, represent, recount, detail, explain, draw

deserve *vb* merit, earn, warrant, justify, rate

destination *n* end, terminus, terminal, station, address, target

destroy *vb* wreck, spoil, demolish, ruin, annihilate, damage, devastate, ravage, raze, level, blight, abolish, break, mutilate ANTONYM: *build*

detail 1. *n* particular, trait, feature, factor, specific, peculiarity, fact, point

2. *vb* specify, describe

dialect *n* idiom, vernacular, patois, slang, lingo, argot, jargon, cant, creole, pidgin accent, language

die 1. *vb* decease, expire, pass away, pass on, perish, succumb, depart, starve ANTONYM: *live*

2. *n* form

different 1. *adj* distinct, other, else, another, separate, dissimilar, unlike, irregular, uneven, unequal, unique ANTONYM: *same, similar*

2. *adj* diverse, various, assorted, miscellaneous, disparate, eclectic, assorted, varied, heterogeneous, motley, many

3. *adj* strange

diplomat *n* ambassador, consul, emissary, statesman, attaché, envoy, minister, chargé d'affaires, official

dirty 1. *adj* filthy, grimy, soiled, dingy, grubby, unclean, impure, unsanitary, contaminated, polluted, foul, dusty, squalid, messy ANTONYM: *clean*

2. *adj* obscene, lewd, pornographic, ribald, vulgar, bawdy, coarse, earthy, salty, risqué, racy, common

3. *vb* soil, stain, sully, pollute, contaminate, infect, defile, tarnish, taint, foul, befoul, smudge, muddy, mess ANTONYM: *clean*

disabled 1. *adj* handicapped, physically challenged, differently abled, impaired, incapacitated

2. *adj* hampered, thwarted, encumbered, deterred, handicapped, disadvantaged, stymied

3. *adj* broken

disagreement *n* contention, friction, discord, strife, dissent, dissension, heresy, argument, contradiction, fight, opposition

disappear *vb* vanish, fade, lift, dissipate, dissolve, evaporate, fizzle, disperse, thin, melt, stop

disappoint *vb* let down, fail, discourage, dishearten, dissatisfy, disillusion, frustrate, sadden

disaster 1. *n* catastrophe, calamity, tragedy, casualty, cataclysm, misfortune, pity, evil, accident, emergency

2. *n* disappointment

discover 1. *vb* detect, unearth, uncover, strike, descry, ferret out, find, notice

2. *vb* learn

disease *n* infection, virus, fever, contagion, blight, syndrome, blight, illness, epidemic

dishonest *adj* untruthful, untrustworthy, deceitful, crooked, lying, deceptive, corrupt, unprincipled, unscrupulous, fake, sly, bad

disobey *vb* defy, disregard, violate, break, misbehave, transgress, rebel, refuse, fight, sin ANTONYM: *obey*

distance 1. *n* stretch, length, interval, gap, way, expanse, extent, measure

2. *n* background

disturb 1. *vb* disarrange, displace, dislocate, disorder, mess, muss, dishevel, rumple, garble, move

2. *vb* interrupt, disrupt, intrude, interfere, impose, bother, distract

3. *vb* agitate, upset, perturb, unnerve, unsettle, disconcert, ruffle, jar, worry, bother

divide 1. *vb* part, split, partition, segment, subdivide, portion, apportion, halve, quarter, zone, cut, separate, share

2. *vb* diverge, branch, fork

3. *vb* arrange

do 1. *vb* accomplish, achieve, carry out, render, act, cause, work

2. *vb* solve

3. *vb* satisfy

document *n* record, certificate, form, file, diploma, citation, affidavit, passport, deed, credentials, manuscript, report, agreement, license, ticket

door *n* doorway, entrance, entry, exit, gate, gateway, access, portal, passage, outlet, opening, mouth, threshold

dream *n* reverie, daydream, trance, daze, spell, stupor, study, swoon hope dress 1. *vb* wear, clothe, don, robe, attire, costume, outfit, deck

2. *vb* trim, groom, array, decorate

3. *vb* bandage

4. *n* gown, frock, jumper, sheath, skirt, shift, shirtwaist, pinafore, smock, sari, sarong, muumuu, clothes

drive 1. *vb* steer, maneuver, navigate, pilot, ride, propel, jockey, operate, control

2. *vb* banish

3. *n* trip

4. *n* ambition, energy

drug *n* antibiotic, narcotic, sedative, tranquilizer, painkiller, anesthetic, opiate, hallucinogen, antidepressant, medicine

dry 1. *adj* arid, parched, dehydrated, dessicated, dusty, thirsty, stale ANTONYM: *wet*

2. *adj* dull

3. *adj* droll, wry, deadpan, sardonic, funny

4. *adj* sour

5. *vb* wipe, drain

6. *vb* evaporate, dehydrate, wilt, wither, shrivel, harden

dull 1. *adj* uninteresting, boring, tedious, dreary, monotonous, tiresome, prosaic, humdrum, shallow, deadly, dry, drab, insipid ANTONYM: *interesting, lively*

2. *adj* slow, stolid, obtuse, dense, unimaginative, square, stupid

3. *adj* blunt, unsharpened ANTONYM: *sharp*

4. *adj* drab, dim, dingy, faded, lackluster, flat, bleak, dark, dim ANTONYM: *bright*

duplicate 1. *n* double, twin, replica, counterpart, equivalent, analog, parallel, copy, model

2. *vb* repeat, reproduce

duty 1. *n* responsibility, obligation, trust, charge

2. *n* job

3. *n* tax

eager *adj* enthusiastic, keen, avid, anxious, ardent, passionate, fervent, exuberant, impatient, ready, ambitious

early 1. *adj* initial, original, first, earliest, pioneering, pioneer, primary, inaugural, introductory, preliminary, incipient, embryonic, developing, nascent ANTONYM: *late*

2. *adj* premature, untimely, precocious, hasty, prompt, sudden ANTONYM: *late*

3. *adj* primitive, primeval, prehistoric, primal, archaic, primordial, old ANTONYM: *modern*

easy *adj* effortless, light, simple, moderate, straightforward, obvious, plain ANTONYM: *hard*

eat 1. *vb* consume, devour, dine, feast, feed, graze, browse, gulp, gobble, wolf, gorge, bolt, prey on

2. *vb* corrode

edge *n* rim, margin, fringe, brink, boundary, verge, brim, lip, hem, periphery, border, circumference, side, shore

educated *adj* literate, learned, knowledgeable, informed, studious, scholarly, erudite, lettered, well-read, well-informed, well-versed, schooled, bookish, smart ANTONYM: *ignorant*

effect 1. *n* result, outcome, consequence, upshot, aftermath, issue, product

2. *n* impact, impression, influence

3. *vb* cause

embarrass *vb* abash, disconcert, rattle, faze, discomfit, fluster, mortify, chagrin, shame emergency *n* crisis, exigency, extremity, disaster, trouble, accident

emotion *n* sentiment, passion, drama, affect, feeling

emphasize *vb* highlight, feature, stress, accent, accentuate, underscore, underline

empty 1. *adj* vacant, unoccupied, uninhabited, bare, austere, blank, void, devoid, hollow, open, abandoned ANTONYM: *full*
2. *adj* idle, vain, meaningless, hollow
3. *vb* unload, unpack, unwrap, remove, dump out, pour out, clean out, evacuate, vacate, deflate, drain

enemy *n* rival, adversary, antagonist, foe, attacker, assailant, opponent

energy 1. *n* vigor, vitality, life, liveliness, pep, stamina, endurance, vim, drive, get-up-and-go, zip, steam, strength, excitement
2. *n* power, horsepower, pressure, thrust, propulsion, voltage, current, electricity, heat, fuel

enough *adj* ample, sufficient, adequate, abundant, plentiful, plenty, much

enter 1. *vb* penetrate, invade, infiltrate, go, approach, intrude ANTONYM: *leave*
2. *vb* board, mount, embark, entrain, enplane ANTONYM: *leave*
3. *vb* join

enthusiasm *n* passion, zeal, fervor, zest, ardor, eagerness, exuberance, gusto, pleasure, excitement, ambition

envy 1. *vb* desire, covet, resent, grudge, begrudge, want
2. *n* jealousy, covetousness, resentment, spite, desire, malice, greed

equal 1. *adj* same, fair
2. *n* peer, fellow, mate, match, compeer, duplicate

erase *vb* obliterate, delete, scratch, eradicate, expunge, efface, abolish escape 1. *vb* flee, elude, evade, dodge, break out, bolt, elope, avoid, leave

2. *n* flight, getaway, evasion, desertion, deliverance, rescue, departure

estimate 1. *vb* calculate, evaluate, approximate, reckon, figure, gauge, assess, judge, appraise, guess

2. *n* approximation, evaluation, appraisal, assessment, estimation, bid, quotation, quote, comparison, budget

event 1. *n* incident, occurrence, episode, circumstance, occasion, happening, phenomenon, actuality, fact

2. *n* milestone, landmark, breakthrough, achievement, experience, adventure, ceremony, disaster

3. *n* game

exaggerate *vb* overstate, overdo, inflate, embellish, embroider, elaborate, gild, magnify, dramatize

exaggeration *n* overstatement, hyperbole, embroidery, embellishment, elaboration

examine 1. *vb* investigate, scrutinize, inspect, probe, scan, study, look

2. *vb* test, quiz, interrogate, ask

example *n* instance, case, illustration, specimen, sample, representation, representative, model

excellence *n* perfection, faultlessness, superiority, greatness, distinction, eminence, majesty

excite *vb* stimulate, exhilarate, agitate, thrill, energize, arouse, galvanize, enliven, fan ANTONYM: *calm*

exclude *vb* eliminate, suspend, reject, omit, eject, skip, neglect, ignore, overlook, miss, remove, rid, banish, bar, forbid, forget

expensive *adj* costly, invaluable, precious, dear, high-priced, overpriced, extravagant, upscale, valuable, rich ANTONYM: *cheap*

experience 1. *n* background, training, knowledge, skill, know-how, expertise, knowledge, wisdom, event

2. *vb* undergo, encounter, endure, live through, bear

expert 1. *n* authority, specialist, master, virtuoso, ace, connoisseur

2. *adj* proficient, skilled, masterly, adroit, ace, versed, well-versed, able, smart

explain *vb* clarify, interpret, justify, demonstrate, elucidate, illustrate, illuminate, exemplify, expound, show, treat, solve, describe

explode *vb* erupt, discharge, detonate, blow up, burst, break

face 1. *n* features, visage, countenance, expression, profile, appearance

2. *n* side

3. *vb* oppose, confront, defy, brave, challenge, encounter, bear, compete, fight ANTONYM: *retreat*

fair 1. *adj* just, impartial, equal, unbiased, equitable, objective, unprejudiced, neutral, nonpartisan, detached, impersonal, right

2. *adj* satisfactory, acceptable, adequate, mediocre, decent

3. *adj* clear, sunny, bright, pleasant, mild, bright ANTONYM: *cloudy*

4. *adj* blond, blonde, light, white, ivory, creamy, bleached, pale

5. *adj* pretty

6. *n* carnival

faithful 1. *adj* loyal, true, devoted, steadfast, constant, trusty, trustworthy, resolute, staunch, fast, unfailing, unshaken, committed, tenacious, reliable, religious ANTONYM: *unfaithful*

2. *adj* correct

fake 1. *adj* false, artificial, imitation, dummy, ersatz, counterfeit, spurious, phony, bogus, sham, mock, dishonest ANTONYM: *real*

2. *n* phony, counterfeit, forgery, imitation, dummy, copy

3. *n* cheat

4. *vb* forge, counterfeit, falsify, imitate, pretend

fall 1. *vb* drop, collapse, plunge, topple, tumble, plummet, slump, plump, crumple, subside, slip, lapse, sink, set, descend, trip, lose

2. *n* tumble, spill, dive, nosedive, drop

3. *n* wig

family 1. *n* relative, relation, kin, people, kindred, lineage, clan, tribe, stock, strain ancestry

2. *adj* familial, domestic, home, homey, household, residential

famous *adj* famed, noted, prominent, renowned, eminent, notorious, celebrated, illustrious, distinguished, well-known, popular, important, great

far 1. *adj* distant, remote, faraway, far-flung, removed, outlying, yonder

2. *adv* considerably, incomparably, notably, greatly, much

farm 1. *n* ranch, homestead, plantation, spread, farmstead

2. *vb* till, harvest, garden, grow

fashion 1. *n* style, trend, fad, craze, rage, mode, vogue, thing

2. *vb* make, form, build

fast 1. *adj* rapid, quick, speedy, swift, fleet, hasty, hurried, prompt, cursory, perfunctory, snap, sudden ANTONYM: *slow*

2. *adj* faithful

3. *adj* tight

4. *adv*, quickly

fat 1. *adj* plump, obese, stout, overweight, corpulent, portly, chubby, brawny, husky, heavyset, stocky, pudgy, squat, big, heavy

2. *n* oil, lard, shortening, tallow, suet, grease

favorite 1. *adj* preferred, favored, pet, choice, best-liked, popular

2. *n* darling, pet, precious, ideal, lover

3. *n* preference

fear 1. *n* alarm, fright, dread, terror, panic, horror, phobia, anxiety, apprehension, foreboding, dismay, consternation, scare, worry

2. *vb* flinch, cower, tremble, quail, quake, dread

feast 1. *n* banquet, fiesta, repast, meal, party

2. *vb* eat

feeling 1. *n* sense, sensation, perception, feel, touch, quality

2. *n* sensitivity, sentimentality, intuition, instinct, heart, soul, warmth, emotion, impulse

3. *n* belief

feminine *adj* female, ladylike, womanly, matronly, effeminate, motherly ANTONYM: *masculine*

few *adj* several, couple, scant, scanty, negligible, sporadic ANTONYM: *many*

field 1. *n* meadow, pasture, clearing, glade, plot, hayfield, cornfield, wheatfield, farmland, pen

2. *n* playing field, athletic field, diamond, gridiron, arena, track, court, stadium, coliseum, gymnasium

3. *n* airfield, airport, battlefield, battleground

4. *n* subject, area, sphere, realm, discipline, province, arena, bailiwick, domain, orbit, department, profession, specialty

fight 1. *vb* battle, struggle, wrestle, grapple, combat, clash, conflict, war, brawl, feud, duel, skirmish, scrap, strive, resist, argue, attack, compete, face

2. *n* battle, engagement, struggle, war, action, strife, conflict, hostilities, warfare, combat, skirmish, confrontation, encounter, violence, competition, game

3. *n* altercation, clash, scuffle, tussle, scrap, melee, brawl, feud, duel, showdown, fray, rumble, argument, disturbance

4. *n* defiance, resistance, opposition, struggle

finally 1. *adv* conclusively, decisively, irrevocably, permanently, certainly
2. *adv* eventually, ultimately, lastly

finish 1. *vb* complete, end, terminate, conclude, attain, expire,
   wind up, finalize, clinch, use up, dissolve, disband, stop, use,
   climax ANTONYM: *start*
2. *n* end, conclusion, ending, finale, completion, termination,
   culmination, death, fulfillment
3. *n* shine, polish, paint, varnish, shellac, lacquer, stain, wax

fire 1. *n* flame, blaze, conflagration, combustion, campfire, bonfire, pyre,
   inferno, holocaust, fireplace
2. *n* gunfire, shooting, firing, shelling, bombardment
3. *vb* shoot
4. *vb* dismiss, discharge, terminate, lay off, let go, sack, oust
   ANTONYM: *hire*

firm 1. *adj* rigid, hard, solid, stiff, inflexible, steady, compact,
   dense, tough, hard, thick
2. *n* business

fix 1. *vb* repair, mend, patch, restore, renovate, renew, rebuild, overhaul,
   recondition, service, adjust, correct, tinker
2. *vb* sterilize
3. *n* trouble

flexible *adj* bendable, limber, supple, lithe, malleable, elastic, pliable,
   plastic, soft, resilient, pliant, limp

flood 1. *n* deluge, torrent, inundation, cascade, rain, storm
2. *n* river, surge, current, rush, flow, stream, tide, wave, fountain
3. *n* barrage, hail, volley, spate, deluge, torrent, storm
4. *vb* inundate, overflow, submerge, drown, engulf, swamp,
   overwhelm, flow

fly 1. *vb* soar, glide, float, drift, wing, hover, sail, flutter

2. *vb* hurry

3. *n* housefly, horsefly, bluebottle, blackfly, fruit fly, bug

4. *n* tent

follow 1. *vb* succeed, ensue, supplant, supersede, replace
ANTONYM: *lead, precede*

2. *vb* pursue, chase, trail, track, shadow, hunt, stalk, hound, tail

3. *vb* obey

4. *vb* know

food *n* nourishment, diet, sustenance, edibles, victuals, refreshment,
rations, provisions, cuisine, fare, nutrition, fuel, board, meal

fool 1. *n* simpleton, nitwit, idiot, dunce, imbecile, nincompoop,
blockhead, moron, oaf, clown, ignoramus, buffoon, dolt, dummy, half-
wit, ninny

2. *vb* outsmart, outwit, outfox, delude, cheat

forbid *vb* prohibit, ban, disallow, outlaw, censor, gag, boycott, proscribe,
sanction, bar, exclude ANTONYM: *let*

force 1. *vb* require, compel, coerce, make, oblige, obligate, impel,
constrain, pressure, insist, order

2. *n* strength

3. *n* army

foreign *adj* alien, imported, exotic, remote, distant, nonnative,
immigrant, strange

forever *adv* always, eternally, permanently, perpetually, interminably,
endlessly, evermore, regularly

forget *vb* neglect, omit, overlook, disregard, misremember, exclude
ANTONYM: *remember*

forgive *vb* excuse, pardon, absolve, acquit, exonerate, clear, vindicate, condone ANTONYM: *blame*

frantic 1. *adj* frenzied, distraught, overwrought, frenetic, desperate, delirious, feverish ANTONYM: *calm*

2. *adj* hectic, chaotic, furious ANTONYM: *calm*

free 1. *vb* release, liberate, emancipate, deliver, discharge, extricate, exempt, loose, loosen, unloose, unloosen, forgive, open

2. *adj* independent, liberated, sovereign, self-governing, autonomous, emancipated, unconfined, unrestrained, unfettered, unshackled, loose, exempt

3. *adj* complimentary, gratis, gratuitous

4. *adj* generous

friend *n* girlfriend, boyfriend, companion, associate, partner, acquaintance, ally, comrade, pal, chum, playmate, buddy, *amigo (Spanish)* ANTONYM: *enemy, opponent*

full 1. *adj* packed, loaded, laden, filled, crowded, stuffed, replete, sated, brimful, crammed, jammed ANTONYM: *empty*

2. *adj* complete

funny 1. *adj* laughable, amusing, humorous, witty, hilarious, comical, comic, ridiculous, whimsical, facetious, antic, farcical, zany, ludicrous, dry, foolish, strange

2. *adj* sick

future 1. *n* hereafter, eternity, futurity, *mañana (Spanish)*, tomorrow, morrow, destiny, fate

2. *adj* imminent, impending, pending, forthcoming, upcoming, approaching, prospective, projected

game *n* sport, pastime, recreation, contest, match, competition, bout, event, meet, tournament, series, fight

gather 1. *vb* collect, assemble, accumulate, amass, compile, congregate, convene, meet, rendezvous, save, pile

2. *vb* pick, harvest, reap, pluck, garner, glean

3. *vb* assume, infer

general 1. *adj* widespread, extensive, comprehensive, common, usual, universal

2. *adj* approximate

generous 1. *adj* unselfish, charitable, liberal, unsparing, altruistic, kind, free, noble ANTONYM: *selfish*

2. *adj* liberal, handsome, lavish, abundant, big

genius 1. *n* prodigy, virtuoso, mastermind, wizard

2. *n* talent

3. *n* soul

gentle 1. *adj* light, mild, soft, tender, moderate, temperate, calm

2. *adj* friendly, kind

3. *adj* docile, meek, tractable, tame

get 1. *vb* obtain, acquire, gain, win, take, procure, earn, score, catch, receive, seize, find

2. *vb* know

3. *vb* persuade

gift 1. *n* present, donation, grant, contribution, endowment, offering, alms, sacrifice, favor, surprise, boon, inheritance, prize

2. *n* talent

give 1. *vb* present, donate, grant, endow, bestow, impart, award, confer, bequeath, contribute, supply ANTONYM: *receive*

2. *vb* pass, hand, deliver, convey, render, serve, dish out, hand over, hand in, submit, dispense, distribute, inflict, offer

3. *vb* have, hold, stage, act, play

4. *vb* surrender

5. *vb* yield, bear, produce, furnish, make

go 1. *vb* progress, proceed, pass, head, advance, forge ahead, leave, move, travel ANTONYM: *come*

2. *vb* act

3. *vb* belong

4. *vb* happen

5. *n* try

god *n* goddess, deity, divinity, demigod, immortal, idol, icon, effigy

good 1. *adj* fine, excellent, outstanding, choice, admirable, splendid, rave, favorable, hopeful, positive, suitable, proper, capital, tiptop, fair, great, nice, cool ANTONYM: *bad*

2. *adj* honest, honorable, virtuous, worthy, respectable, reputable, moral, righteous, scrupulous, kind

3. *adj* obedient, well-behaved, dutiful, well-mannered, respectful, obliging, polite ANTONYM: *rude*

4. *n* welfare

government *n* administration, legislature, congress, senate, parliament, assembly, regime, rule

grade *n* class, rank, step, score, standing, position, degree, plateau, level, state, slant

gratitude *n* appreciation, thankfulness, thanks, gratefulness, recognition, acknowledgment

great 1. *adj, interj* wonderful, terrific, superb, remarkable, astounding, incredible, spectacular, tremendous, marvelous, fabulous, super, heavenly, good, grand, nice

2. *adj* famous

3. *adj* big

greedy *adj* selfish, possessive, covetous, acquisitive, avaricious, stingy, rapacious, grasping, voracious, insatiable, gluttonous, jealous, predatory

group 1. *n* gang, bunch, crew, pack, set, class, band, body, cluster, ring, bloc, clique, syndicate, junta, troop, troupe
2. *n* band

grow 1. *vb* sprout, germinate, develop, expand, increase, mature, ripen, evolve, enlarge, wax, magnify, amplify, heighten, augment, mushroom, multiply, prosper, blossom, strengthen
2. *vb* raise, breed, cultivate, nurture, rear, plant

guarantee 1. *vb* insure, assure, secure, ensure, warrant, certify, promise
2. *n* promise

guess *vb* suppose, think, believe, imagine, suspect, reckon, speculate, surmise, estimate, assume

guide 1. *n* conductor, escort, leader, usher, shepherd, pilot
2. *n* pattern
3. *vb* lead

guilty *adj* culpable, blameworthy, responsible, liable, derelict
ANTONYM: *innocent*

gun *n* firearm, weapon, pistol, revolver, sidearm, handgun, rifle, carbine, shotgun, machine-gun, musket, flintlock, muzzle loader, blunderbuss, cannon, arms

habit 1. *n* custom, practice, routine, institution, usage, rule
2. *n* dependency, addiction, instinct, reflex, wont, tendency
3. *n* mannerism, affectation, quirk, trait, oddity
4. *n* clothes

habitat *n* environment, habitation, ecosystem, den, house

hang 1. *vb* dangle, drape, suspend, swing, hover, depend

2. *vb* lynch, execute, kill

happen *vb* occur, transpire, chance, go, befall, ensue, arise, recur, exist

happy *adj* glad, cheerful, joyful, joyous, merry, gay, jolly, delighted, gleeful, proud, jovial, high, festive, bright, ecstatic, satisfied, lucky ANTONYM: *sad*

hard 1. *adj* stony, rocky, adamant, firm, tough

2. *adj* difficult, tough, demanding, strenuous, arduous, rigorous, heavy, rough, trying ANTONYM: *easy*

3. *adj* harsh, severe, bitter, austere, stark, stern

harm 1. *n* injury, hurt, loss, impairment, detriment, disadvantage, abuse, damage

2. *vb* hurt, damage

hate 1. *vb* detest, abhor, despise, deplore, loathe, disdain, dislike, abominate, scorn, execrate ANTONYM: *love*

2. *n* hatred

heal *vb* cure, remedy, mend, knit, treat, medicate, nurse, doctor

health *n* fitness, condition, shape, vigor, vitality, haleness, wellness, healthfulness, welfare

heaven 1. *n* paradise, bliss, nirvana, elysian fields, Elysium, Valhalla, utopia, pleasure

2. *n* air

heavy 1. *adj* cumbersome, hefty, ponderous, massive, weighty, bulky, big ANTONYM: *light*

2. *adj* serious

3. *adj* hard

height 1. *n* altitude, elevation, stature, loftiness, tallness ANTONYM: *depth*
2. *n* top

help 1. *vb* assist, aid, serve, wait on, cooperate, collaborate, team up, succor, benefit, improve, enrich, avail, relieve, support
2. *n* aid, assistance, cooperation, relief, service, support, comfort, generosity, welfare
3. *n* worker

herd *n* flock, pack, swarm, hive, colony, bevy, brood, school, gaggle, pod, group, crowd

hesitate *vb* falter, vacillate, balk, pause, demur, equivocate, waver, stop, delay, wait

hide 1. *vb* conceal, disguise, secrete, bury, withhold, hoard, squirrel (away) ANTONYM: *reveal*
2. *vb* cover (up), camouflage, obscure, eclipse, mask, block, screen, shade, shroud, veil, cloak, cover
3. *n* pelt, skin, fleece, fell, rawhide, chamois, coat

high 1. *adj* tall, lofty, towering, soaring, big
2. *adj* high-pitched, shrill, treble, piping, loud ANTONYM: *low*
3. *adj* important
4. *adj* happy

hill 1. *n* knoll, mound, hillock, foothill, down, dune, bank, ridge, pile, mountain, cliff ANTONYM: *valley*
2. *n* slant

hit 1. *vb* strike, pound, batter, beat, maul, bash, bump, pelt, smash, smack, swat, hammer, buffet, pat, punch, knock, collide, whip
2. *n* blow

hole 1. *n* hollow, cavity, pit, crater, abyss, chasm, crevasse, cave, den, well

2. *n* puncture, perforation, opening, aperture, vent, crack, cleft, fissure, crevice, split, gap, rupture, leak, pore

home 1. *n* house, apartment, condominium, dwelling, residence, abode, domicile, habitation, cabin, cottage, bungalow, chalet, mansion, palace, manor, villa, chateau, den, shack

2. *n* family

3. *n* base

4. *n* hospital

honesty *n* candor, frankness, veracity, truth, virtue

hope 1. *vb* wish, expect, anticipate, aspire, believe, want, intend

2. *n* desire, faith, longing, aspiration, dream, ambition

3. *n* virtue

horizon *n* skyline, limit, range, border

hospital *n* infirmary, clinic, medical center, rehabilitation center, sanatorium, sanitarium, nursing home, home

hot 1. *adj* scalding, boiling, broiling, roasting, sizzling, sweltering, torrid, warm, burning, tropical ANTONYM: *cold*

2. *adj* spicy

3. *adj* fashionable

huge *adj* enormous, immense, gigantic, prodigious, colossal, tremendous, mighty, vast, gross, gargantuan, monstrous, jumbo, mammoth, massive, titanic, big

human being *n* human, person, individual, being, soul, body, mortal, hominid, humanity, man, woman, people

humble 1. *adj* meek, modest, unassuming, unpretentious, self-deprecating, self-effacing, shy ANTONYM: *proud*

2. *adj* common

3. *vb* condescend

hungry *adj* starving, starved, famished, ravenous, underfed, malnourished, undernourished, emaciated, wasted

hunt 1. *vb* fish, shoot, poach, track, follow

2. *vb* search, seek, look, investigate, scour, forage, probe, ransack, rummage, delve, explore, prospect, comb, sift

3. *n* search, investigation, pursuit, chase, quest, exploration, study

hurry 1. *vb* rush, hasten, hustle, speed, race, hurtle, accelerate, quicken, scurry, sally, dash, zip, whiz, zoom, scamper, scuttle, surge, swarm, pour, stampede, storm

2. *n* rush, haste, scramble, stampede, speed

hurt 1. *vb* injure, afflict, damage, wound, bruise, tear, wrench, twist, dislocate, harm, abuse, hit, insult, punish, break, pull

2. *vb* smart, sting, burn, irritate, ache, throb, tingle

hypocrite *n* deceiver, faker, dissembler, quack, con artist, cheat

ice *n* frost, hail, sleet, icicle, ice cube, permafrost

idea *n* thought, concept, impression, inspiration, notion, inkling, belief, theory, plan, suggestion

ignorant *adj* illiterate, uneducated, unlearned, unlettered, unschooled, unread, naive, stupid, unaware ANTONYM: *educated*

illegal *adj* unlawful, illegitimate, illicit, criminal, outlawed, wrongful, prohibited, taboo

illness *n* sickness, ailment, malady, affliction, disorder, infirmity, complaint, disease, nausea

imaginary *adj* unreal, nonexistent, fictional, fictitious, illusory, hypothetical, fanciful, hallucinatory, legendary ANTONYM: *real*

imagine 1. *vb* conceive, picture, see, envision, envisage, visualize, fancy, fantasize, pretend

2. *vb* guess, think

imitate *vb* copy, mimic, emulate, simulate, parrot, ape, parody, mock, lampoon, satirize, impersonate, caricature

immoral *adj* unethical, unprincipled, shameless, dissolute, degenerate, depraved, perverted, bad, wrong

important 1. *adj* significant, principal, chief, major, main, essential, primary, critical, key, paramount, prime, cardinal, foremost, high, weighty, urgent, necessary, valuable, meaningful, memorable, predominant
2. *adj* influential, prominent, powerful, famous

impossible 1. *adj* inconceivable, unattainable, unthinkable, incomprehensible, useless, illogical, unbelievable
2. *adj* insoluble, unsolvable, inexplicable, unexplainable, unaccountable
3. *adj* intolerable

inability *n* incapability, ineptitude, incompetence, incapacity, inefficacy, impotence, powerlessness, failure

incompetent *adj* incapable, inept, ineffectual, unqualified, unfit, inefficient, unable, amateur, clumsy

infer *vb* deduce, conclude, gather, judge, reason, ascertain, assume, mention

infinite *adj* boundless, unbounded, endless, limitless, unlimited, interminable, countless, immeasurable, inexhaustible, eternal, big ANTONYM: *finite*

innocent 1. *adj* blameless, guiltless, faultless, sinless, pure, chaste, angelic, impeccable ANTONYM: *guilty*
2. *adj* naive

insane *adj* crazy, mad, crazed, lunatic, psychotic, maniacal, demented, deranged, berserk, paranoid, unbalanced, unhinged ANTONYM: *sane* insensitive *adj* unfeeling, uncaring, tactless, heartless, hardhearted, coldhearted, callous, unsympathetic, cold-blooded, thoughtless, apathetic, stubborn ANTONYM: *thoughtful*

inside 1. *adj* interior, internal, inner, indoor, innermost, middle
2. *n* middle

insist *vb* demand, require, assert, argue, order, force

instead *adv* rather, alternatively, alternately, preferably

insult 1. *vb* offend, humiliate, slander, defame, malign, smear, slight, snub, outrage, tease, taunt, scorn abuse, hurt, ridicule
2. *n* affront, offense, indignity, outrage, slander, libel, smear, jeer

intellectual *adj* scholarly, scholastic, educational, academic, cerebral, mental, profound, thoughtful

interesting *adj* fascinating, intriguing, stimulating, engrossing, absorbing, engaging, entertaining, provocative, stirring, compelling, exciting ANTONYM: *dull*

introduce 1. *vb* present, acquaint, familiarize, inform, apprise, broach
2. *vb* preface, precede, start

invent 1. *vb* devise, design, develop, conceive, formulate, originate, contrive, hatch, improvise, ad-lib, build, discover, form, make, start
2. *vb* fabricate, concoct, make up, counterfeit, lie

invisible *adj* imperceptible, indiscernible, undetectable, concealed, hidden, unseen, microscopic, impalpable, ethereal, supernatural, inconspicuous

irony *n* sarcasm, satire, incongruity, parody, humor

island *n* isle, islet, atoll, key, cay, archipelago, holm

jail 1. *n* prison, penitentiary, correctional facility, jailhouse, reformatory, cell, dungeon, brig, stockade

2. *vb* imprison, confine, detain, incarcerate, impound, remand, institutionalize, commit

jealous *adj* envious, resentful, possessive, begrudging, suspicious, greedy

job *n* task, chore, work, duty, errand, assignment, project, mission, labor, living, profession, function

join 1. *vb* connect, associate, attach, link, fasten, unite, couple, interlock, anchor, bridge, buckle, clasp, clinch, knit, pair, graft, weld, solder, cement, pin, tie, unify, marry
2. *vb* enter, enroll, enlist, register, participate

joke 1. *n* prank, practical joke, gag, caper, antic, trick
2. *n* jest, wisecrack, pun, witticism, quip, one-liner, bon mot, story
3. *vb* jest, quip, banter, spar, kid, tease, josh

judge 1. *n* justice, magistrate, jurist
2. *n* referee, umpire, official, evaluator, reviewer, critic, arbiter
3. *vb* decide
4. *vb* estimate, infer

jump 1. *vb n* leap, spring, bound, vault, hop, pounce, bounce, jounce, jolt, pop, skip, hurdle, dive, plunge, lunge, dance
2. *vb n* start, flinch, wince, recoil, twitch, jerk, cringe, cower

justice 1. *n* fairness, impartiality, equity, due process, evenhandedness, honesty, truth, virtue
2. *n* judge

keep 1. *vb* have, possess, maintain, retain, preserve, sustain, own
2. *vb* save
3. *vb* fulfill, honor, respect, celebrate
4. *n* board
5. *n* castle, tower

kill *vb* murder, slay, assassinate, dispatch, massacre, butcher, execute, slaughter, exterminate, annihilate, eradicate, martyr, sacrifice, destroy, extinguish, choke

kind 1. *adj* compassionate, considerate, benevolent, well-meaning, charitable, merciful, kindhearted, tenderhearted, warmhearted, decent, kindly, benign, humane, friendly, generous, loving, nice, tolerant
2. *n* type

king *n* monarch, sovereign, maharajah *(India)*, rajah *(India)*, sultan *(Muslim)*, shah *(Iran)*, pasha *(Turkey, N. Africa)*, khan *(central Asia, China)*, sachem *(Native American)*, ruler, emperor

knot 1. *n* tangle, snarl, snag, hitch, splice
2. *vb* tie

know *vb* understand, realize, recognize, apprehend, comprehend, see, fathom, grasp, follow, get, penetrate, remember

knowledge *n* fact, information, learning, data, evidence, education, awareness, erudition experience, wisdom, education

label 1. *n* tag, sticker, ticket, tab, marker, insignia, trademark, logo, service mark, brand, name
2. *vb* mark, ticket, name
3. *vb* stereotype

last 1. *adj* latest, final, ultimate, extreme, concluding, closing, terminal, hindmost, outermost, latter
2. *vb* continue

late 1. *adj* overdue, tardy, belated, delayed, delinquent ANTONYM: *early, punctual*
2. *adj* new
3. *adj* dead
4. *adv* behind, behindhand, belatedly, tardily

laugh *vb n* giggle, chuckle, snicker, roar, guffaw, snigger, titter, cackle, howl, shriek, smile

layer *n* stratum, tier, sheet, level, film, membrane, coat

lazy *adj* indolent, idle, shiftless, slothful, apathetic, listless ANTONYM: *ambitious*

lead 1. *vb* guide, direct, conduct, usher, steer, take, send, show, funnel, bring ANTONYM: *follow*

2. *vb* direct, manage, supervise, administer, run, preside, oversee, chair, officiate, control, govern, command ANTONYM: *follow*

3. *n* front

learn 1. *vb* ascertain, realize, discover, determine, see, find, find out

2. *vb* memorize, absorb, assimilate, master, digest, study, remember, practice

least *adj* smallest, tiniest, minutest, slightest, minimal, minimum, merest ANTONYM: *best*

leave 1. *vb* depart, exit, embark, withdraw, desert, abandon, vacate, evacuate, forsake, quit, maroon, strand, set out, set off, flee, defect, go, move ANTONYM: *enter, wait*

2. *vb* disembark, detrain, deplane, land, descend ANTONYM: *enter*

3. *vb* will, bequeath, bestow, hand down, give

4. *n* vacation

legal *adj* lawful, legitimate, permissible, statutory, prescribed, allowable, licit, constitutional, sanctioned, valid, official ANTONYM: *illegal*

legendary *adj* mythical, mythological, fabulous, fabled, apocryphal, traditional, proverbial, imaginary

less 1. *adj* fewer, smaller, diminished, reduced, lower ANTONYM: *more*

2. *prep* minus

lesson *n* class, teaching, drill, exercise, homework, assignment, education let 1. *vb* allow, permit, authorize, license, tolerate, enable, entitle, qualify, empower, agree ANTONYM: *prevent*

2. *vb* hire

level 1. *adj* flat, smooth, even, flush, parallel, trim, straight

2. *adj* plane, horizontal, flat, low

3. *n* grade, layer, floor

4. *vb* destroy

5. *vb* even, smooth, flatten, grade, plane, straighten

liar *n* fibber, storyteller, deceiver, prevaricator, perjurer, falsifier, equivocator, cheat

lie 1. *n* falsehood, fib, untruth, fiction, story, tale, fabrication, invention, deception, disinformation, misrepresentation, concoction, canard, pretense, dishonesty ANTONYM: *truth*

2. *vb* deceive, fib, prevaricate, falsify, mislead, dissemble, misstate, equivocate, fabricate, invent, pretend

3. *vb* rest, recline, repose, sprawl, loll

life 1. *n* being, animation, vitality, breath, sentience, consciousness, living, existence

2. *n* lifetime, longevity, span, career

3. *n* energy

light[1] 1. *n* radiance, illumination, luminosity, brilliance, brightness, glare, glow, sheen, glimmer, shine, gleam, luster, gloss, glitter, twinkle, sparkle, glint

2. *n* day

3. *n* lamp, lightbulb, bulb, streetlight, lantern, chandelier, flashlight, torch

4. *n* ray, beam, beacon, flash, flare, signal, spark

5. *adj* bright

6. *adj* fair

7. *vb* illuminate, light up, illumine, brighten, lighten

8. *vb* ignite, kindle, strike, fuel, burn

light² 1. *adj* lightweight, underweight, slight, slender, scant, sparse, buoyant, weightless, insubstantial ANTONYM: *heavy*

2. *adj* gentle

3. *adj* easy

4. *vb* descend

like 1. *vb* enjoy, be fond of, care for, relish, fancy, delight in, love, appreciate

2. *adj* alike, same

link 1. *n* connection, association, contact, bond, correlation, attachment, tie, joint, affinity, affiliation, bridge, junction, union

2. *vb* join

list 1. *n* catalog, program, schedule, agenda, outline, menu, roster, inventory, table

2. *vb* itemize, record, catalogue, inventory, register, tabulate, enumerate, specify

3. *vb* slant

listen *vb* hear, hearken, hark, overhear, eavesdrop, attend

live¹ 1. *vb* exist, be, thrive, subsist, breathe, experience

2. *vb* survive, outlive, outlast, persevere, persist, continue ANTONYM: *die*

3. *vb* reside, dwell, stay, abide, inhabit, lodge, room, sojourn, occupy

live² *adj* lively, alive, active

loan 1. *n* credit, advance, mortgage, rental, accommodation, allowance

2. *vb* lend

lonely *adj* lonesome, homesick, solitary, friendless, outcast, alone, sad long 1. *adj* lengthy, tall, extended, elongated, outstretched, extensive, big ANTONYM: *short*

2. *adj* lengthy, protracted, unending, long-winded, sustained

3. *vb* want

look 1. *vb* watch, glance, observe, witness, view, regard, spy, sight, eye, survey, peek, see, stare, examine

2. *vb* seem, appear, resemble

3. *vb* hunt

4. *n* glance, peek, view, gaze, glimpse, scrutiny, inspection

5. *n* appearance

lose 1. *vb* misplace, mislay, drop, miss, forget ANTONYM: *find*

2. *vb* succumb, fall, fail, surrender ANTONYM: *win*

loud 1. *adj* noisy, resounding, deafening, thunderous, earsplitting, piercing, resonant, strident, shrill, audible, high ANTONYM: *quiet*

2. *adj* boisterous, rowdy, rambunctious, raucous, vociferous, clamorous, obstreperous, stentorian, cacophonous, uproarious, rude

3. *adj* garish, flashy, gaudy, showy, ostentatious, tacky, bright, fancy

love 1. *vb* adore, cherish, admire, worship, idolize, dote on, revere, like, court ANTONYM: *hate*

2. *n* affection, devotion, fondness, passion, tenderness, adoration, attachment, infatuation, kindness, desire, virtue ANTONYM: *hate*

3. *n* lover, beloved, darling, dear, sweetheart, girlfriend, boyfriend, fiancé (male), fiancée (female)

4. *n* zero *(in tennis)*

loyalty *n* allegiance, fidelity, faithfulness, devotion, fealty, dependability, dedication, patriotism

luck *n* windfall, godsend, opportunity, break, success, chance magic 1. *adj* enchanted, charmed, magical, mystical, occult, bewitching, entrancing, spellbinding, lucky, mysterious

2. *n* sorcery, witchcraft, wizardry, enchantment, hocus-pocus, voodoo

make 1. *vb* create, make up, manufacture, produce, fashion, model, compose, constitute, forge, strike, build, form, invent

2. *vb* force

3. *vb* earn

4. *n* brand, model, brand name, type

man *n* gentleman, boy, guy, fellow, husband, male, chap, lad, human being, humanity, adult

manufactured *vb* made, machine-made, manmade, mass-produced, synthetic, artificial, human-made

many 1. *adj* numerous, various, countless, manifold, diverse, multiple, innumerable, sundry, myriad, different ANTONYM: *few*

2. *n* abundance

masculine *adj* male, manly, virile, macho, gentlemanly, fatherly ANTONYM: *feminine*

matter 1. *n* substance, material, body, element, constituent, stuff

2. *n* subject

3. *n* business

4. *n* trouble

5. *vb* count, signify, imply, mean

maybe *adv* perhaps, possibly, conceivably, feasibly, perchance, probably

mean 1. *adj* cruel, vicious, malicious, merciless, savage, malignant, ruthless, brutal, low, cold-blooded, inhuman, relentless, pitiless, unkind, violent, revengeful

2. *adj* small-minded, petty, selfish, intolerant, prejudiced, greedy ANTONYM: *tolerant*

3. *adj* middle

4. *n* average

5. *vb* signify, indicate, symbolize, connote, denote, imply, spell, matter, intend, suggest

measure 1. *n* dimension, distance, capacity, weight, volume, mass, amount, number, size, speed

2. *n* rule, gauge, scale, standard, criterion, benchmark, yardstick, touchstone

3. *n* rhythm

4. *vb* weigh, gauge, rule, time

medicine 1. *n* medication, prescription, pill, tablet, capsule, ointment, lotion, injection, shot, vaccine, cure, drug

2. *n* medical science, medical profession, healing, science

meeting 1. *n* appointment, engagement, date, rendezvous, tryst, encounter, confrontation, run-in, brush

2. *n* conference, assembly, gathering, reunion, convention, council, interview, session, talk

3. *n* introduction

4. *n* junction

melt *vb* dissolve, thaw, liquefy, fuse, evaporate, soften, disappear

member 1. *n* affiliate, constituent, fellow, enrollee, colleague, participant, partner

2. *n* limb

memory *n* recollection, reminiscence, recall, remembrance, déjà vu mention 1. *vb* refer to, touch on, infer, allude, state, name, specify, say, suggest, broach

2. *n* remark

messy *adj* untidy, disorderly, sloppy, slovenly, disheveled, bedraggled, unkempt, dirty ANTONYM: *neat*

method *n* approach, procedure, process, technique, system, routine, manner, way, plan

middle 1. *n* center, core, midpoint, hub, nucleus, focus, midst, interior, inside, soul, depth, essence

2. *adj* central, inner, interior, median, mean, midmost, intermediate, inside, average

miracle *n* wonder, marvel, phenomenon, rarity, oddity, portent

mischievous *adj* naughty, disobedient, unruly, wayward, spoiled, ill-behaved, impish, elfish, elfin, rude, rebellious, bad ANTONYM: *good*

misery *n* suffering, agony, anguish, distress, grief, pain, torment, torture, heartache, hardship, sorrow

mistake 1. *n* error, slip, blunder, oversight, faux pas, inaccuracy, fallacy, miscalculation, fault, defect, misunderstanding

2. *vb* misunderstand

misunderstand *vb* misinterpret, misjudge, misconstrue, mistake, err

mix 1. *vb* combine, blend, merge, mingle, compound, consolidate, stir, whip, beat, knead, roll, churn, jumble, scramble, shuffle, join

2. *vb* associate, mingle, intermingle, socialize, fraternize, consort, join

3. *n* assortment

model 1. *n* paragon, ideal, archetype, exemplar, paradigm, nonpareil, standard, prototype, original, example

2. *n* miniature, representation, reduction, mock-up, copy, duplicate

3. *n* make, pattern

4. *n* subject, sitter, fashion model, poser, mannequin

5. *vb* make

6. *vb* pose, sit, show

7. *adj* classic, outstanding, first-rate, excellent, authoritative, typical, archetypal, definitive, perfect

modern 1. *adj* contemporary, current, up-to-date, stylish, recent, modernistic, newfangled, space-age, state-of-the-art, latter-day, new

2. Modern *adj* art

moment 1. *n* instant, point, minute, second, twinkling, wink, jiffy, flash, trice, time, period

2. *n* importance

money *n* cash, currency, coin, revenue, capital, specie, wealth, property

mood *n* humor, morale, temper, temperament, disposition, spirits, vein, state, setting

more 1. *adj* additional, extra, added, further, supplementary, another, new ANTONYM: *less*

2. *adv* additionally, furthermore, still, yet, better, preferably, sooner, rather

3. *n* increase, supplement, extra, surplus

most 1. *adj* maximum, utmost, greatest

2. *n* majority, maximum, bulk, preponderance

3. *adv* very, best

move 1. *vb* shift, remove, budge, dislodge, carry, push

2. *vb* transfer, relocate, migrate, emigrate, immigrate, leave, go, travel

3. *vb* affect

4. *vb* suggest

much 1. *adv* greatly, enormously, extremely, dearly, very, far

2. *adj* enough, abundant

3. *n* abundance

murder 1. *n* homicide, manslaughter, assassination, bloodshed, massacre, slaughter, slaying, carnage, annihilation, crime

2. *vb* kill

mysterious *adj* puzzling, enigmatic, perplexing, baffling, inexplicable, uncanny, mystic, mystical, magic, strange, obscure

myth *n* legend, fable, epic, lore, folklore, tradition, mythology, story, superstition

naive *adj* unsophisticated, inexperienced, simple, innocent, artless, ingenuous, trusting, green, gullible, credulous, unaware, amateur, harmless

native 1. *adj* indigenous, aboriginal, endemic, original, domestic, local, homegrown, natural

2. *n* citizen

natural 1. *adj* organic, pure, unprocessed, raw, uncooked, plain, normal

2. *adj* inborn, inherent, instinctive, innate, hereditary, inherited, congenital, genetic, intrinsic, native

nausea *n* indigestion, queasiness, vomiting, sickness, qualm, illness

near 1. *adj* close, nearby, immediate, intimate, imminent, local, adjacent, about, approximate

2. *adj* future

3. *prep* beside

4. *vb* approach

neat *adj* tidy, trim, orderly, organized, shipshape, precise, spruce, clean, prim, legible ANTONYM: *messy* necessary *adj* essential, indispensable, basic, required, requisite, fundamental, mandatory, compulsory, obligatory, imperative, important

need 1. *vb* require, lack, want
2. *vb* must, should, ought, have
3. *n* necessity, reason
4. *n* hardship, poverty

negotiate *vb* mediate, moderate, bargain, referee, confer, transact, haggle, parley, intercede, arbitrate, decide

neighborhood *n* community, block, vicinity, quarter, precinct, ward, borough, place, zone

nervous *adj* restless, fidgety, shaky, edgy, uptight, skittish, self-conscious, jittery, jumpy, high-strung, afraid, anxious, cowardly

new 1. *adj* fresh, original, recent, late, latest, novel, brand-new, trendy, up-to-date, unused, unspoiled, pristine, virgin, untouched, modern ANTONYM: *old*
2. *adj* more

nice 1. *adj* agreeable, delightful, fantastic, good, great, pleasant
2. *adj* good-natured, charming, pleasant, agreeable, affable, good-humored, thoughtful, polite, friendly, kind
3. *adj* careful

noble 1. *adj* royal, aristocratic, highborn, patrician, titled, blue-blooded, princely, kingly, regal, imperial, elite
2. *adj* worthy, generous, magnanimous, courtly, chivalrous, chivalric, grand, good
3. *n* nobleman, noblewoman, aristocrat, peer, lord, lady

noise *n* sound, din, uproar, clamor, racket, hubbub, tumult, commotion, pandemonium, hullabaloo, peal, bang, cry, peep normal *adj* typical, average, natural, standard, conventional, common, usual

notice 1. *vb* observe, note, perceive, discover, look, see

2. *n* attention, observation, regard, heed, note, publicity, warning

3. *n* advertisement, announcement, reminder

now *adv* immediately, straightaway, directly, right away, instantly, quickly, soon

number 1. *n* numeral, figure, digit, cipher, integer, fraction

2. *n* amount, quantity, batch, lot, bunch, bundle, group, assortment

3. *n* act

obey *vb* comply, mind, follow, heed, behave, adhere, observe, meet ANTONYM: *disobey*

object 1. *vb* protest, disagree, dissent, oppose, dispute, disapprove, frown, argue, complain, contradict ANTONYM: *agree*

2. *n* thing, article, item, gadget, device

3. *n* objective, purpose, aim, goal, sake, target, intention, intent, ambition

obvious *adj* clear, evident, apparent, transparent, noticeable, overt, glaring, blatant, gross, conspicuous, prominent, palpable, pronounced, marked, distinct, patent, bald, easy, plain ANTONYM: *obscure*

offer 1. *vb* propose, present, tender, bid, proffer, extend, suggest, quote, give, sell

2. *n* suggestion, invitation

official 1. *adj* authentic, authorized, legitimate, approved, licensed, valid, formal, real, correct

2. *n* leader, administrator, executive, bureaucrat, civil servant, public servant, boss, judge

often *adv* frequently, repeatedly, oftentimes, recurrently, regularly, usually ANTONYM: *seldom*

old 1. *adj* elderly, aged, venerable, mature, senior, hoary, seasoned ANTONYM: *young*

2. *adj* ancient, old-fashioned, antique, archaic, antiquated, obsolete, outdated ANTONYM: *new*

3. *adj* worn, used, run-down, worn-out, secondhand, decrepit, shabby, ragged

only 1. *adv* just, barely, hardly, scarcely, merely, simply, exclusively

2. *adj* single, sole, solitary, unique, one, lone

open 1. *adj* ajar, uncovered, unfastened, unlocked, accessible, unobstructed, unsealed

2. *adj* spacious, deserted, clear, empty

3. *vb* unfasten, undo, unbolt, untie, free, clear, separate

4. *vb* start

operate *vb* function, perform, run, drive, act, work, use

opponent *n* rival, competitor, opposition, challenger, antagonist, adversary, foe, competition, contestant, enemy ANTONYM: *friend*

opportunity *n* chance, occasion, excuse, opening, situation, luck

opposite 1. *adj* opposing, contradictory, contrary, conflicting, inverse, converse, reverse, contrasting, antithetical, counter, different

2. *adj* facing, opposed, fronting, confronting

3. *n* reverse, contrary, converse, antithesis, inverse

4. *prep* facing, across from, against, opposed to, versus

optimistic *adj* hopeful, confident, cheerful, sanguine, expectant, bullish, idealistic, certain ANTONYM: *pessimistic* order 1. *vb* command, direct, instruct, decree, bid, dictate, impose, prescribe, ordain, mandate, ask, tell, insist, force

2. *vb* arrange, straighten

3. *n* arrangement, formation, organization, layout, disposition, alignment, placement, sequence, succession, system, plan

4. *n* decree, command, commandment, demand, ultimatum, direction, directive, charge, mandate, edict, behest, writ

5. *n* religion

organization 1. *n* association, corporation, institution, foundation, society, club, fraternity, sorority, business, union, group

2. *n* order

outside 1. *n* exterior, surface, façade

2. *adj* exterior, external, outer, outermost, outward, outdoor, alfresco

3. *adv* outdoors, out-of-doors, out, alfresco

own 1. *vb* possess, hold, have, retain, maintain, enjoy, occupy, keep

2. *vb* admit

3. *adj* private

page 1. *n* sheet, leaf, folio

2. *n* intern, servant

3. *vb* call

pain 1. *n* suffering, discomfort, ache, pang, soreness, twinge, stitch, spasm, cramp, sting

2. *n* misery

3. *n* nuisance

pair 1. *n* couple, duo, twosome, twins, brace *(of animals)*, yoke *(of oxen)*, span *(of horses)*, team

2. *vb* join

paper 1. *n* stationery, notepaper, writing paper, newsprint, crepe paper, tissue, wax paper, tar paper, parchment, vellum

2. *n* document, report

3. *n* newspaper, magazine, journal, periodical, tabloid, gazette, daily, weekly

parade 1. *n* procession, march, demonstration, cavalcade, motorcade

2. *vb* walk, strut

3. *vb* advertise

parallel 1. *adj* equidistant, collateral, aligned, even, alongside, abreast, level

2. *adj* alike

3. *n* duplicate, similarity

4. *vb* compare

part 1. *n* piece, section, portion, segment, fragment, fraction, share, element, facet, aspect, component, ingredient, content, bit, block, division ANTONYM: *total*

2. *vb* divide, separate

3. *n* role, function

partner 1. *n* associate, co-worker, confederate, accomplice, accessory, sidekick, helper

2. *n* friend

3. *n* love, spouse

party 1. *n* celebration, festivity, gathering, reception, soiree, fete, occasion, gala, function, revelry, jubilee, merrymaking, feast

2. *n* faction, bloc, league, lobby, junta, cabal, organization, group

3. *n* participant, litigant, principal, member, contestant

4. *vb* celebrate

past 1. *adj* former, preceding, foregoing, prior, previous, antecedent, old

2. *adj* finished, over, ended, through, done

3. *n* history, antiquity, yesterday, yesteryear, yore

4. *prep* beyond, through, behind, over, after

path *n* pathway, footpath, trail, track, lane, walk, walkway, runway, shortcut, road, course

patient 1. *adj* understanding, forbearing, mild-tempered, long-suffering, tolerant, calm, passive

2. *adj* persistent, persevering, steadfast, assiduous, diligent

3. *n* subject, victim, sufferer, convalescent, invalid, outpatient, inpatient

patriotic *adj* loyal, zealous, nationalistic, chauvinistic, faithful

pattern 1. *n* design, motif, configuration, structure, plan

2. *n* model, blueprint, template, diagram, guide, sketch

3. *vb* form

pay 1. *vb* compensate, recompense, spend, reward, tip, remunerate, settle, disburse, expend, atone, expiate, give, earn, refund

2. *n* wage

pen 1. *n* corral, fold, pound, paddock, enclosure, coop, cage, sty, stall, kennel, barn, field, jail

2. *n* ballpoint, marker, fountain pen, quill, nib

3. *vb* write

people 1. *n* citizenry, populace, public, population, society, civilization, community, folk, hoi polloi *(Greek),* bourgeoisie *(French),* human being, humanity, citizen

2. *n* family

perfect 1. *adj* ideal, flawless, faultless, impeccable, unblemished, immaculate, exquisite, exemplary, model, correct, infallible

2. *adj* pure, sheer, outright, complete

3. *vb* polish, hone, amend, fix, correct

period 1. *n* interval, term, span, spell, duration, extent, stretch, streak, cycle, bout, season, phase, stage, time, shift, watch, tour, stint, round, moment

2. *n* age, eon, era, epoch, date

permanent *adj* durable, lasting, enduring, abiding, perennial, persistent, indelible, continual, eternal, stationary ANTONYM: *temporary*

permission *n* consent, authorization, authority, approval, license, sanction, support

personality 1. *n* character, disposition, temperament, temper, nature, identity

2. *n* charisma, charm, presence, allure, magnetism, bearing, attraction

3. *n* celebrity

perspective *n* point of view, viewpoint, standpoint, orientation, direction, angle, position, attitude, side, view

persuade *vb* convince, satisfy, influence, induce, dispose, coax, sway, get, wheedle, cajole, entice, prevail, snow, urge, tempt ANTONYM: *discourage*

pessimistic *adj* cynical, negative, glum, sullen, morose, fatalistic, bleak, sad ANTONYM: *optimistic*

physical *adj* bodily, corporal, corporeal, fleshly, real

picture 1. *n* portrait, image, drawing, painting, illustration, representation, diagram, sketch, cartoon, poster, work, plate, print, description, photograph, X ray

2. *n* movie

3. *vb* imagine

4. *vb* draw

pile 1. *n* heap, stack, mound, hill, lump, wad, clump, mass, nugget, bulk, assortment

2. *vb* heap, stack, gather

3. *n* post

pioneer 1. *n* settler, homesteader, backwoodsman, frontiersman, immigrant, colonist, colonizer

2. *n* creator

3. *adj* early

pirate 1. *n* buccaneer, privateer, freebooter, corsair, plunderer, marauder, criminal, vandal

2. *vb* steal

pity 1. *n* sympathy, compassion, empathy, mercy, forbearance, ruth, clemency, condolence, commiseration, kindness, comfort

2. *vb* sympathize, commiserate, comfort

3. *n* disaster

place 1. *n* location, position, situation, locale, site, spot, locality, region, vicinity, space, zone

2. *vb* locate, situate, assign, store, put

3. *vb* arrange

4. *n* house

5. *n* profession

plain 1. *adj* simple, uncomplicated, unadorned, unvarnished, frugal, severe, austere, stark, common, humble, natural, naked ANTONYM: *complicated*

2. *adj* unattractive, homely, drab, unlovely, ugly ANTONYM: *pretty*

3. *adj* obvious, straightforward

4. *n* prairie, range, grassland, savanna, heath, moor, tundra, downs, field, plateau

plan 1. *n* design, project, plot, schematic, outline, map, table

2. *n* aim, intent, goal, purpose, strategy, scheme, plot, conspiracy, program, policy, platform, plank, provision, method, recipe

3. *vb* plot, scheme, conspire, contrive, connive, chart, map, outline, arrange, prepare, intend

planet *n* heavenly body, celestial body, satellite, earth, space

plant 1. *n* shrub, weed, grass, bush, vegetation, flora, foliage, organism, flower, tree, herb, vegetable, fruit

2. *n* factory

3. *vb* seed, sow, pot, transplant, propagate, set, broadcast, scatter, grow

4. *vb* put

plateau 1. *n* tableland, table, mesa, steppe, upland, highland, plain

2. *n* grade

play 1. *vb* frisk, sport, disport, romp, frolic, gambol, recreate

2. *vb* compete

3. *vb* perform, finger, bow, strum, practice, blow

4. *vb* act

5. *vb* run, show, present, air, broadcast

6. *n* recreation, horseplay, clowning, pleasure, entertainment

7. *n* drama, dramatization, skit, pageant, tragedy, melodrama, comedy, farce, musical, mystery, program, movie

8. *n* movement

please *vb* delight, gratify, gladden, content, hearten, satisfy, entertain, pamper

poison 1. *n* venom, toxin, bane, infection, virus, germ

2. *vb* kill

polite *adj* courteous, well-mannered, civil, chivalrous, gracious, friendly, thoughtful, nice, prim ANTONYM: *rude*

pompous *adj* grandiloquent, flowery, grandiose, bombastic, pretentious, turgid, condescending, proud

poor 1. *adj* needy, penniless, destitute, broke, impoverished, deprived, indigent, poverty-stricken ANTONYM: *rich*

2. *adj* pitiful, sorry, paltry, inferior, shoddy, deficient, pedestrian, tawdry, unsatisfactory, inadequate, worthless, wretched, abject, lame

possession 1. *n* ownership, custody, title, proprietorship, receipt, control, rule

2. *n* property, acquisition

3. *n* colony

possible *adj* plausible, conceivable, believable, credible, feasible, potential, reasonable, imaginable, practicable, viable, likely

poverty *n* destitution, want, need, penury, indigence, privation, impoverishment, hardship

practical 1. *adj* matter-of-fact, down-to-earth, realistic, reasonable, rational, sensible, unsentimental, able ANTONYM: *impractical*

2. *adj* useful, efficient

3. *adj* virtual

practice 1. *vb* rehearse, drill, train, study, learn

2. *vb* use

3. *n* rehearsal, repetition, preparation, discipline

4. *n* habit

praise 1. *n* applause, acclaim, compliment, approval, adulation, acclamation, kudos, congratulations, flattery, respect

2. *vb* commend, extol, acclaim, laud, compliment, honor, decorate, congratulate, toast, rave, celebrate, clap, flatter, worship

predict *vb* forecast, foretell, prophesy, prognosticate, project, divine, tell, foresee, augur, portend, presage, anticipate

prefer *vb* favor, endorse, advocate, choose, like, want

prejudice *n* intolerance, bigotry, bias, partiality, predisposition, predilection, favoritism, discrimination, racism, sexism, chauvinism, ageism, hatred

prepare *vb* develop, provide, ready, plan, adapt, prime, process, refine, arrange, cook, make, invent

pretend *vb* feign, affect, simulate, profess, act, assume, imagine, lie, fake

pretty *adj* lovely, handsome, attractive, good-looking, fair, becoming, comely, striking, beautiful, cute ANTONYM: *ugly*

prevent *vb* avert, hinder, forestall, check, restrain, thwart, foil, frustrate, deter, inhibit, stunt, hobble, leash, stop, block, discourage, contain ANTONYM: *let*

prey 1. *n* quarry, victim, target
2. *vb* eat
3. *vb* cheat

price *n* charge, expense, cost, fare, payment, amount, fee, consideration, outlay, worth, bill

pride 1. *n* self-respect, self-esteem, dignity, self-confidence, respect
2. *n* vanity, conceit, arrogance, vainglory, egotism, hubris, narcissism, haughtiness
3. *n* pleasure

primitive 1. *adj* basic
2. *adj* early
3. *adj* uncivilized, simple, crude, rough, rustic, unsophisticated, untamed, aboriginal, pristine

print 1. *vb* publish, issue, reprint, write

2. *vb* imprint, impress, engrave, stamp, emboss, inscribe

3. *n* etching, engraving, woodcut, lithograph, photocopy, photograph, picture

4. *n* impression, imprint, indentation, fingerprint, footprint, track

5. *n* text, printing, type, typescript, writing

prisoner *n* captive, inmate, detainee, internee, slave, hostage

private 1. *adj* secluded, isolated, remote, withdrawn, insular, quarantined

2. *adj* personal, individual, intimate, own ANTONYM: *public*

3. *adj* exclusive, restricted, reserved, special ANTONYM: *public*

4. *adj* secret

probably *adv* presumably, apparently, plausibly, seemingly, maybe

problem 1. *n* mystery, puzzle, riddle, dilemma, enigma, ambiguity, conundrum, contradiction, question

2. *n* trouble

profession *n* occupation, employment, appointment, vocation, avocation, calling, career, livelihood, post, position, situation, place, craft, trade, job, field, business, specialty

program 1. *n* performance, concert, recital, show, production, broadcast, telecast, presentation, series, play, movie, entertainment

2. *n* list

3. *n* plan, course

progress 1. *n* improvement, progression, headway, advance, advancement, momentum, movement, growth, success

2. *vb* go

promise 1. *n* oath, vow, word, pledge, assurance, commitment, covenant, guarantee

2. *vb* swear, pledge, vow, assure, warrant, guarantee

proof *n* evidence, testimony, verification, certification, documentation, data, corroboration, confirmation, substantiation, authentication

property 1. *n* possessions, belongings, effects, goods, assets, holdings, capital, things, stuff, wealth, acquisition

2. *n* land, lot, estate, yard, grounds, premises, plot, tract

3. *n* quality

protect 1. *vb* defend, guard, shield, safeguard, fortify, watch, mind, tend, save, patrol ANTONYM: *attack*

2. *vb* shelter, cover, cushion, pad

protest 1. *n* demonstration, strike, sit-in, teach-in, rally, complaint

2. *vb* demonstrate, picket, strike, walk out, complain, object

3. *vb* complain, object, argue

proud 1. *adj* egotistic, conceited, vain, arrogant, egocentric, haughty, smug, superior, pretentious, pompous ANTONYM: *humble*

2. *adj* grand

3. *adj* happy

pull 1. *vb* tow, drag, haul, draw, tug, yank, jerk, pluck, attract, bring, tighten, strain, extract ANTONYM: *push*

2. *vb* sprain, strain, hurt

3. *n* tug, yank, drag, jerk, wrench, attraction

punctual *adj* timely, prompt, precise, expeditious, punctilious ANTONYM: *late*

punish *vb* discipline, penalize, sentence, correct, fine, abuse, hurt, hit, scold, whip punishment *n* penalty, sentence, penance, deserts, retribution, consequence, discipline, abuse

push 1. *vb* press, shove, impel, thrust, jostle, nudge, elbow, shoulder, shove, slide, thrust, prod, poke, ram, jam, wedge, move, force ANTONYM: *pull*

2. *vb* urge

3. *n* blow, impulse

put *vb* set, lay, park, deposit, plant, position, implant, install, insert, place

quality *n* property, characteristic, character, trait, attribute, air, atmosphere, texture, tone, class, feeling

question 1. *n* query, inquiry, interrogation, interrogative, problem ANTONYM: *answer*

2. *n* doubt

3. *n* subject

4. *vb* ask

quickly *adv* speedily, hastily, hurriedly, fast, rapidly, expeditiously, instantaneously, promptly, headlong, now, soon

quiet 1. *adj* silent, still, hushed, noiseless, soundless, inaudible, mute, mum, speechless, low ANTONYM: *loud*

2. *n* calm

3. *vb* hush, silence, soften, mute, muffle, stifle, muzzle, gag

quote 1. *vb* cite, repeat, parrot, paraphrase, recite, declaim, render, mention, say, tell

2. *n* estimate

race 1. *n* run, dash, sprint, relay, marathon, footrace, horse race, steeplechase, derby, game

2. *vb* run, hurry

3. *n* type

4. *n* humanity

rain 1. *n* precipitation, shower, downpour, drizzle, cloudburst, torrent, storm

2. *vb* pour, drizzle, sprinkle, shower, teem, precipitate

range 1. *n* extent, scope, spread, reach, compass, sweep, spectrum, assortment, space, horizon

2. *n* plain

3. *vb* wander

4. *vb* spread

rare *adj* uncommon, scarce, infrequent, occasional, special, valuable

read 1. *vb* peruse, skim, scan, browse, study

2. *vb* comprehend, decipher, decode, perceive

3. *vb* indicate, register, record, show

ready 1. *adj* prepared, set, qualified, ripe, equipped, available

2. *adj* willing, disposed, predisposed, eager, likely

3. *vb* prepare

real 1. *adj* actual, material, tangible, substantive, concrete, objective, solid, true, palpable, physical ANTONYM: *imaginary*

2. *adj* actual, genuine, authentic, bona fide, veritable, literal, legitimate, pure, natural ANTONYM: *fake*

really 1. *adv* actually, genuinely, literally, indeed, veritably, certainly

2. *adv* very

reason 1. *n* purpose, cause, motive, explanation, call, grounds, need, rationale, necessity, incentive, justification

2. *n* logic, reasoning, thinking, induction, deduction, analysis, wisdom

3. *vb* think, infer

4. *n* sanity, mental health, lucidity, saneness

rebel 1. *vb* revolt, mutiny, resist, defy, face, dare

2. *n* revolutionary, insurgent, mutineer, subversive, dissident, freedom fighter, traitor, turncoat, extremist

receive 1. *vb* accept, admit, take, inherit, greet, get ANTONYM: *give, refuse*

2. *vb* welcome, entertain

recently *adv* lately, newly, just, latterly

reflect 1. *vb* echo, mirror, ricochet, rebound, bounce

2. *vb* consider, meditate

refund 1. *vb* reimburse, repay, remit, compensate, pay

2. *n* reimbursement, repayment, compensation, rebate

refuse 1. *vb* deny, reject, decline, dismiss, disapprove, spurn, repudiate, rebuff, snub, scorn, flout, deprive, repel

2. *n* trash

regret 1. *vb* repent, apologize, bewail, bemoan, lament, deplore, rue, grieve

2. *n* compunction, repentance, disappointment, sorrow, shame

regularly *adv* constantly, invariably, always, ever, continually, habitually, routinely, religiously, naturally, typically, often, usually, forever

relationship *n* relation, kinship, affinity, rapport, compatibility, link, friendship

relevant *adj* pertinent, germane, apposite, applicable, apropos, related, relative, fit

reliable *adj* dependable, trustworthy, responsible, reputable, unimpeachable, solid, conscientious, sure, surefire, faithful, able, indisputable

religion 1. *n* faith, mythology, theology, religiosity, spirituality, orthodoxy, belief, philosophy

2. *n* denomination, sect, order, cult

reluctant *adj* hesitant, unwilling, grudging, disinclined, loath, averse, diffident, squeamish

remember *vb* recall, recollect, reminisce, remind, recognize, commemorate, memorialize, know, learn ANTONYM: *forget*

repair 1. *n* adjustment, improvement, renovation, restoration, patch, plug, mend, service, servicing, correction

2. *vb* fix

repeat 1. *vb* redo, replicate, duplicate, reduplicate, reproduce

2. *vb* recur, reoccur

3. *vb* reiterate, restate, recapitulate, echo, rehearse, rehash, recount, quote

report 1. *n* essay, paper, composition, theme, treatise, thesis, dissertation, article, announcement, speech, story, study

2. *n* bang

3. *vb* tell

reproduce 1. *vb* copy, duplicate, photocopy, clone, imitate

2. *vb* procreate, breed, propagate, multiply, proliferate, generate, beget, spawn, hatch

resemble *vb* look like, take after, match, approximate, favor, correspond

respect 1. *n* admiration, honor, reverence, dignity, homage, esteem, regard, estimation, deference, courtesy, awe, wonder, prestige, pride

2. *vb* esteem, admire, revere, value, prize, cherish, appreciate

3. *vb* keep

rest 1. *vb* relax, repose, unwind, recuperate, lounge, loaf, laze, idle, sleep, lie

2. *vb* depend

3. *n* relaxation, repose, ease, sleep, break, vacation

4. *n* remainder

return 1. *vb* come back, go back, revisit, recur, reoccur, resurface, reappear, rebound, renew

2. *n* arrival, homecoming, reappearance, recurrence, reoccurrence, resurgence

3. *n* recovery, restoration, restitution, reimbursement, repayment

4. *n* wage

revenge 1. *n* vengeance, retaliation, repayment, compensation, satisfaction, vindication

2. *vb* avenge, retaliate, repay, requite, vindicate

revolution 1. *n* rebellion, revolt, insurrection, uprising, coup, coup d'état, insurgence, treason, disturbance

2. *n* change

3. *n* circle

rich 1. *adj* wealthy, affluent, prosperous, well-to-do, moneyed, well-off, comfortable, posh, successful ANTONYM: *poor*

2. *adj* opulent, resplendent, ornate, lavish, lush, luxurious, profuse, grand, fashionable, expensive, fancy

3. *adj* sweet, sugary, creamy, buttery, fattening, luscious, succulent, cloying, saccharine, honeyed, delicious

4. *n* aristocracy

right 1. *n* power, privilege, prerogative, authority, license, freedom

2. *adj* correct, fit, fair ANTONYM: *wrong*

3. *adv* correctly

4. *adv* soon

5. *adv* precisely

road *n* street, avenue, boulevard, thoroughfare, artery, roadway, lane, alley, highway, path

rough 1. *adj* coarse, uneven, rugged, irregular, bumpy, jagged, crumpled, rumpled, harsh, scratchy, hoarse

2. *adj* choppy, raging, ruffled, wild, stormy

3. *adj* rude, primitive

4. *adj* hard

5. *adj* approximate

rude *adj* impolite, insolent, discourteous, ungracious, impertinent, impudent, fresh, uncouth, crude, coarse, crass, bold, brash, presumptuous, audacious, sassy, forward, surly, pert, flip, disrespectful, irreverent, cheeky, abrupt, cross, thoughtless ANTONYM: *polite*

rule 1. *n* law, regulation, custom, principle, axiom, guideline, code, precept, canon, ultimatum, act, habit

2. *n* command, control, authority, mastery, sway, sovereignty, charge, government, jurisdiction, dominion, leadership

3. *n* measure

4. *vb* govern

5. *vb* decide

ruler *n* potentate, prince, lord, governor, leader, president, premier, prime minister, king, queen, emperor, empress, dictator

rumor *n* gossip, hearsay, scandal, talk

run 1. *vb* jog, trot, dash, sprint, bolt, dart, streak, gallop, lope, canter, hurry, race

2. *vb* escape, leave

3. *vb* lead

4. *vb* operate

5. *vb* play

6. *vb* flow

7. *n* race

sad *adj* unhappy, miserable, depressed, gloomy, dismal, melancholy, blue, downhearted, downcast, dejected, despondent, doleful, forlorn, moody, down, low, bad, glum, lonely, pitiful, sorry, thoughtful, pessimistic ANTONYM: *happy*

safe 1. *adj* secure, protected, harmless, snug, guarded, impregnable, invulnerable, immune, invincible ANTONYM: *dangerous*

2. *n* vault, strongbox, chest, coffer, treasury, safe-deposit box, cash register

sale 1. *n* deal, transaction, purchase, marketing, auction, trade

2. *n* bargain, deal, clearance, closeout, discount

same *adj* identical, equal, equivalent, corresponding, matching, uniform, consistent, like, alike ANTONYM: *different*

sarcastic *adj* scornful, snide, ironic, ironical, satiric, satirical, sardonic, caustic, derisive

satisfy 1. *vb* appease, slake, quench, sate, satiate, please, relieve, pacify

2. *vb* persuade

3. *vb* suffice, serve, do, fulfill, answer

save 1. *vb* keep, preserve, conserve, maintain, hoard, stockpile, stash, gather ANTONYM: *discard, abolish, waste*

2. *vb* rescue, deliver, salvage, spare, free, protect

3. *vb* bank

4. *pre* but

say *vb* state, speak, remark, exclaim, phrase, verbalize, express, signify, air, vent, dictate, talk, tell, pronounce, reveal

scary *adj* frightening, frightful, dreadful, terrifying, terrible, horrifying, unnerving, appalling, fearful, awesome

secret 1. *adj* hidden, arcane, cryptic, esoteric, mysterious, anonymous

2. *adj* clandestine, confidential, classified, top secret, private, covert, undercover, surreptitious, underground, sly

3. *n* mystery, confidence, intrigue, problem

see 1. *vb* behold, discern, observe, perceive, notice, glimpse, spot, remark, look

2. *vb* know, learn

3. *vb* imagine

sell *vb* carry, stock, retail, handle, trade (in), market, peddle, vend, barter, hawk, offer

send 1. *vb* dispatch, transmit, mail, post, e-mail, forward, convey, ship, transfer, export, spread, broadcast

2. *vb* lead

3. *vb* throw

sense 1. *n* sensation, function, capability, feeling, ability

2. *n* wisdom

3. *n* meaning

serious 1. *adj* solemn, grave, somber, earnest, sedate, sober, heavy, important, profound, dignified

2. *adj* sincere

setting *n* environment, surroundings, framework, background, context, backdrop, scenery, climate, ambiance, mood, medium, milieu

shake 1. *vb* vibrate, tremble, shudder, shiver, quiver, quake, quaver, flutter, wobble, wag, waggle, pulsate, throb, jar, tingle

2. *vb* spread

3. *n* vibration

shame 1. *n* disgrace, dishonor, discredit, humiliation, remorse, regret, contrition, embarrassment, chagrin, guilt

2. *vb* humiliate, dishonor, disgrace, debase, abase, demean, discredit, embarrass

share 1. *n* division, percentage, allowance, allotment, stake, quota, ration, proportion, fraction, percent, ratio, part, interest

2. *vb* distribute, apportion, split (up), deal out, ration, mete out, divide, budget

sharp 1. *adj* keen, acute, honed, pointed, pointy, sharp-edged, knife-edged

2. *adj* smart

3. *adj* acute, abrupt, rapid, sudden

4. *adj* steep

5. *adj* severe, biting, caustic, bitter, harsh, cutting, fierce, brutal, oppressive

6. *adj* spicy, sour

7. *adj* smelly

8. *adj* fashionable

shine 1. *vb* radiate, beam, sparkle, gleam, glow, shimmer, glisten, twinkle

2. *vb* polish, burnish, buff, wax, scour, clean, finish

3. *n* light[1]

shock 1. *vb* astound, appall, dismay, devastate, overwhelm, stun, electrify, stagger, awe, horrify, surprise, scare

2. *n* blow, vibration

3. *n* earthquake

4. *n* blow, upset, jolt, ordeal, trauma, surprise

5. *n* lock

short 1. *adj* slight, low, undersized, skimpy, brief, small ANTONYM: *long*

2. *adj* brief, concise, compact, succinct, abbreviated, terse, laconic, abridged, fleeting, transient, short-lived, fast, temporary

3. *adj* abrupt

4. *adj* inadequate

show 1. *vb* display, exhibit, present, manifest, produce, reveal, advertise, model

2. *vb* lead

3. *vb* explain, verify

4. *n* spectacle, display, play, movie, program

shy *adj* bashful, timid, meek, retiring, diffident, reserved, demure, deferential, timorous, tentative, humble

sick 1. *adj* ill, ailing, sickly, unwell, unhealthy, nauseous, nauseated, queasy, infirm, indisposed, funny, weak ANTONYM: *healthy*

2. *adj* gruesome

sign 1. *n* symbol, signal, token, omen, clue, index, indication, manifestation, symptom, gesture, expression, track, warning

2. *vb* autograph, inscribe, endorse, countersign, initial, write

sincere *adj* genuine, honest, heartfelt, wholehearted, true, trustworthy, serious, straight, straightforward

sink 1. *vb* submerge, submerse, swamp, engulf, immerse, duck, dunk, dip, descend, fall, flood

2. *n* washbasin, basin, lavatory, washstand, bowl

size *n* magnitude, mass, volume, bulk, quantity, proportion, capacity

slavery *n* bondage, servitude, enslavement, serfdom, subjugation, vassalage ANTONYM: *freedom* slow 1. *adj* leisurely, gradual, sluggish, deliberate, moderate, torpid ANTONYM: *fast*

2. *adj* dilatory, lackadaisical, passive, lazy, listless

3. *adj* dull, stupid

small 1. *adj* little, tiny, miniature, minute, diminutive, Lilliputian, compact, trivial ANTONYM: *big*

2. *adj* scanty, meager, slight, spare, skimpy, stingy, paltry, inadequate

smart 1. *adj* intelligent, clever, bright, wise, learned, brilliant, keen, acute, quick, alert, apt, astute, perceptive, insightful, discerning, incisive, canny, shrewd, precocious, educated, profound ANTONYM: *foolish, stupid*

2. *adj* fashionable

3. *vb* hurt

smell 1. *n* scent, odor, aroma, fragrance, perfume, incense, bouquet, stench

2. *vb n* sniff, whiff, scent, sense

3. *vb n* stink, reek

sneak 1. *vb* creep, slink, prowl, skulk, steal, tiptoe, lurk

2. *n* rascal

soldier *n* fighter, warrior, volunteer, conscript, draftee, recruit, cadet, veteran, officer, serviceman, servicewoman, combatant, mercenary, soldier of fortune, gladiator, army, troop

soon *adv* presently, shortly, forthwith, momentarily, anon, quickly, now

sorry 1. *adj* sorrowful, repentant, apologetic, contrite, penitent, remorseful, sad

2. *adj* forlorn, wretched, depressing, sad, pitiful

3. *adj* poor

source 1. *n* origin, derivation, birthplace, cradle, fountain, fountainhead, font, fount, well, wellspring

2. *n* beginning, cause

space 1. *n* universe, cosmos, heavens, outer space, infinity, void, air

2. *n* room, area, scope, range, expanse, territory, elbowroom

special 1. *adj* distinct, particular, specific, especial, distinctive, respective, proper, certain, unique

2. *adj* select, choice, extraordinary, exceptional, unusual, peculiar, remarkable, noteworthy, phenomenal, outstanding, rare, striking, strange

speech 1. *n* voice, communication, discourse, intercourse, utterance, articulation, diction, locution, enunciation, expression, talk, language, remark, accent, dialect

2. *n* lecture, talk, sermon, address, report, oration

speed 1. *n* velocity, acceleration, swiftness, pace, rate, tempo, rapidity, celerity, dispatch, hurry

2. *vb* hurry

spot 1. *n* speck, dot, mark, taint, stain, blot, blemish, blotch, smudge

2. *n* place

3. *n* trouble

4. *vb* find, see

spread 1. *vb* distribute, disseminate, disperse, circulate, strew, shake, sprinkle, scatter, send, broadcast

2. *vb* extend, stretch, range, unfold, expand, widen, gape, yawn

3. *vb* cover

4. *vb* rub

5. *n* growth

6. *n* range

7. *n* farm

8. *n* feast

9. *n* flow

spying *n* espionage, surveillance, intelligence, counterespionage, counterintelligence

stare *vb* gaze, peer, gape, ogle, gawk, look

start 1. *vb* begin, commence, initiate, cause, activate, launch, originate, stem, inaugurate, introduce, innovate, open, trigger, touch off, spark, continue ANTONYM: *finish, stop*

2. *n* beginning

3. *vb* jump

state 1. *n* condition, circumstance, situation, status, stage, phase, grade

2. *n* territory, province, dominion, commonwealth, country, colony, zone

3. *vb* mention, say, tell

steal 1. *vb* rob, swipe, snatch, shoplift, purloin, embezzle, burglarize, rifle, poach, pinch, pilfer, pocket, plagiarize, pirate, filch, take, seize, pillage

2. *vb* sneak

3. *n* bargain

stereotype 1. *n* convention, generalization, categorization, characterization, cliché

2. *vb* categorize, pigeonhole, characterize, label, generalize

stick 1. *vb* poke, jab, probe, stab, plunge, pierce, prick, spear, puncture, lance, gore, peck, penetrate, perforate, riddle, hit

2. *vb* adhere, cohere, glue, paste, tape, cling, cleave, join

3. *n* branch, limb, twig, stem, stalk, staff, stave, wand, cane, club, baton, bar, bat

stop 1. *vb* halt, pause, cease, terminate, brake, arrest, check, stem, discontinue, lift, finish ANTONYM: *start*

2. *vb* prevent, bar

3. *vb* close

storm 1. *n* tempest, gale, rainstorm, snowstorm, blizzard, hailstorm, ice storm, hurricane, typhoon, cyclone, monsoon, tornado, nor'easter, squall, rain, wind, snow

2. *n* flood

3. *vb* attack

4. *vb* hurry

story 1. *n* narrative, account, history, saga, chronicle, tale, narration, anecdote, yarn, plot, scenario, version, report, myth, joke, description

2. *n* lie

3. *n* floor

straight 1. *adj* direct, undeviating, even, unbent, regular, linear, true, level, vertical ANTONYM: *bent, zigzag*

2. *adj* sincere

strange 1. *adj* unfamiliar, unusual, unknown, unaccustomed, outlandish, foreign, new ANTONYM: *common*

2. *adj* odd, peculiar, curious, abnormal, eccentric, quaint, queer, weird, eerie, bizarre, unnatural, ludicrous, different, irregular, mysterious, funny

strengthen 1. *vb* intensify, magnify, amplify, increase, expand, enhance, enlarge, boost, augment, swell, grow

2. *vb* fortify, brace, buttress, reinforce, harden, support

stress 1. *n* pressure, tension, strain, duress, worry

2. *n* accent

3. *vb* emphasize

strong 1. *adj* powerful, mighty, almighty, hardy, stalwart, robust, muscular, vigorous, athletic, virile, burly, tough, invincible, healthy ANTONYM: *weak*

2. *adj* solid, sturdy, durable, sound, substantial, tough

3. *adj* potent, powerful, formidable, violent, forceful, intense

4. *adj* smelly

structure 1. *n* composition, arrangement, shape, form, pattern

2. *n* building

3. *vb* arrange

stubborn *adj* obstinate, headstrong, pertinaceous, dogged, opinionated, obdurate, tenacious, pigheaded, unrelenting, unruly, intractable, difficult, perverse, unmanageable, mulish, ornery, resolute, dogmatic, wild

student *n* pupil, learner, scholar, disciple, schoolchild, schoolgirl, schoolboy, freshman, sophomore, junior, senior, undergraduate, trainee, apprentice

study 1. *vb* analyze, evaluate, think through, pore over, review, research, criticize, survey, poll, canvass, examine, consider, learn, read

2. *n* examination, analysis, investigation, inquiry, exploration, survey, poll, census, sampling, probe

3. *n* report

4. *n* den

5. *n* dream

stupid *adj* ignorant, unintelligent, vacuous, foolish, dull, thoughtless ANTONYM: *smart*

subject 1. *n* theme, topic, question, substance, matter, thesis, gist, point, text, issue, field

2. *n* course

3. *n* model, patient

4. *n* citizen

5. *vb* control

subtract *vb* deduct, remove, withhold, diminish, decrease ANTONYM: *add*

success *n* accomplishment, achievement, attainment, progress, prosperity, victory, luck

sudden *adj* immediate, abrupt, swift, meteoric, precipitate, instantaneous, unexpected, unforeseen, sudden, sharp, early

suggest 1. *vb* recommend, urge, propose, advise, counsel, move, submit, prescribe, offer

2. *vb* imply, hint, intimate, insinuate

summary *n* outline, synopsis, abstract, paraphrase, condensation, abridgment, digest, précis, rundown, essence

supply 1. *n* stock, store, stockpile, inventory, reserve, hoard, cache, mine, holding, account, fund, reservoir

2. *vb* provide, equip, outfit, furnish, provision, rig, give, sell

support 1. *vb* bear, hold (up), bolster (up), brace, sustain, prop (up), buttress, carry, nourish, nurture, feed, promote, foster, strengthen

2. *vb* uphold, sustain, maintain, champion, enforce, back, help, approve

3. *vb* afford

4. *n* backing, encouragement, assistance, succor, maintenance, livelihood, subsistence, upkeep, resource, help, protection, approval, permission, incentive, pension ANTONYM: *opposition*

5. *n* mainstay, pillar, backer, champion, patron, fan

6. *n* brace, prop, buttress, stay, bolster, truss, reinforcement, base, basis

surprise 1. *vb* startle, amaze, astonish, daze, dazzle, bedazzle, flabbergast, throw, floor, shock

2. *n* amazement, astonishment, wonder, incredulity, shock

3. *n* gift

surrender 1. *vb* yield, concede, submit, resign, relinquish, sacrifice, acquiesce, capitulate, quit, give (in), bow, accede, defer, succumb, relent, lose, abandon

2. *n* submission, capitulation, resignation, acquiescence, concession, abdication, renunciation, forfeit, sacrifice

suspicious 1. *adj* distrustful, wary, leery, paranoid, apprehensive, jealous

2. *adj* suspect, queer, shady, dubious, doubtful, strange

swing 1. *vb* sway, rock, oscillate, vibrate, fluctuate, undulate, wave, roll, wobble, pitch, lurch, reel, waddle, turn

2. *vb* wave, brandish, flourish, wield, whirl, twirl

3. *vb* hang

4. *n* rhythm, music

tact *n* judgment, poise, diplomacy, savoir faire, discretion, delicacy, circumspection, finesse

take 1. *vb* convey, deliver, transport, carry, bring, lead

2. *vb* get, receive

3. *vb* confiscate, appropriate, expropriate, commandeer, usurp, gain, seize, catch

4. *vb* ingest, swallow, eat, drink

5. *vb* bear

6. *vb* choose

7. *vb* take in, earn

talent *n* gift, aptitude, genius, skill, expertise, flair, knack, prowess, adroitness, facility, ability, agility, specialty, art

talk 1. *vb* speak, converse, discuss, chat, communicate, confer, consult, parley, rap, argue, chatter, say, tell

2. *n* conversation, discussion, dialogue, consultation, word, chat, chitchat, patter, prattle, gibberish, speech, rumor, meeting

tax 1. *n* duty, tariff, toll, levy, fee, assessment, tribute
2. *vb* tire

teach *vb* instruct, educate, train, school, tutor, coach, lecture, inform, drill, enlighten, explain, preach

team 1. *n* squad, company, unit, crew, side, group
2. *n (in reference to horses, mules, or oxen)* pair, span, yoke, string, tandem

tell *vb* report, narrate, relate, recite, declare, inform, announce, disclose, communicate, convey, notify, state, profess, pronounce, tattle, say, talk, order, warn, testify, predict

temporary *adj* transitory, fleeting, momentary, ephemeral, provisional, stopgap, makeshift, interim, acting, short ANTONYM: *permanent*

term 1. *n* word
2. *n* semester, trimester, quarter, tenure, period
3. *n* qualification, limitation, condition, restriction, stipulation, reservation, clause

theory *n* hypothesis, conjecture, speculation, supposition, premise, presumption, assumption, surmise, idea, reason, philosophy

therefore *adv* consequently, hence, accordingly, thus, ergo, wherefore, for, so

thick 1. *adj* dense, compact, close, condensed, packed, impenetrable, profuse ANTONYM: *thin*
2. *adj* stiff, firm, viscous, syrupy, gelatinous, glutinous, viscid
3. *adj* broad

thin 1. *adj* flimsy, slim, slender, sheer, delicate, diaphanous, insubstantial, gossamer, weak ANTONYM: *thick, heavy*
2. *adj* narrow

3. *adj* slender, slim, lean, slight, skinny, scrawny, lanky, lank, wiry, spare, gaunt, haggard, emaciated ANTONYM: *big, tough*

4. *vb* weaken, disappear

think 1. *vb* reason, deliberate, cogitate, consider, meditate, believe

2. *vb* guess

thoughtful 1. *adj* considerate, sympathetic, tactful, solicitous, sensitive, friendly, polite, kind, nice ANTONYM: *thoughtless*

2. *adj* meditative, contemplative, pensive, reflective, wistful, sad, absorbed, intellectual

thoughtless *adj* inconsiderate, careless, reckless, wanton, heedless, rash, foolhardy, ungrateful, thankless, unappreciative, rude, abrupt, indiscriminate, negligent ANTONYM: *thoughtful*

throw 1. *vb* pitch, toss, hurl, fling, cast, pass, heave, chuck, sling

2. *vb* project, propel, launch, catapult, emit, radiate, send, give off, shoot

3. *vb* confuse, surprise

4. *vb* defeat

5. *n* toss, pitch, pass, cast

ticket 1. *n* pass, admission, voucher, permit, visa, passport, receipt, sales slip, slip

2. *n* ballot

3. *n, vb* label

tie 1. *vb* fasten, secure, knot, bind, lash, tether, hitch, lace, strap, join, link

2. *n* necktie, bow tie, cravat, ascot

3. *n* draw, deadlock, stalemate, standoff

tired 1. *adj* exhausted, weary, worn out, sleepy, fatigued, listless, drained, dead

2. *adj* trite

together 1. *adv* jointly, mutually, collectively, en masse, cooperatively ANTONYM: *apart*

2. *adv* simultaneously, concurrently, contemporaneously

tool 1. *n* instrument, utensil, machine, appliance, gadget, implement, device, mechanism, apparatus, means, vehicle, medium, equipment, hammer

2. *n* instrument, pawn, puppet, stooge, dupe, victim

top 1. *n* peak, summit, pinnacle, apex, apogee, zenith, crest, tip, surface, climax, acme, prime, ultimate ANTONYM: *base*

2. *n* cover, lid, cap, hood, stopper, cork, plug, bung

3. *adj* best

4. *vb* defeat, exceed

total 1. *n* sum, whole, aggregate, amount, totality, entirety, all ANTONYM: *part*

2. *adj* all, complete

3. *vb* add

touch 1. *vb* feel, handle, caress, manipulate, paw, clutch, grope, rub

2. *vb* contact, meet, reach, border

3. *vb* concern

4. *n* feeling, sense

5. *n* bit

tough 1. *adj* sturdy, durable, stout, unbreakable, rugged, resilient, firm, strong

2. *adj* hard

3. *n* bully, vandal

town *n* city, village, municipality, township, hamlet, community, borough, suburb, metropolis, megalopolis, settlement, neighborhood trade 1. *vb* exchange, swap, barter, switch, substitute, interchange, traffic, trade in, sell, change

2. *n* exchange, swap, switch, substitution, sale

3. *n* business, profession

translate *vb* convert, interpret, decipher, decode, paraphrase, render, transcribe, transliterate, paraphrase, transform

trash *n* garbage, rubbish, refuse, waste, debris, litter, rubble, flotsam, wreckage, junk

travel 1. *vb* journey, voyage, tour, cruise, trek, commute, explore, traverse, roam, visit, sail, go, wander

2. *n* passage, transportation, traffic, transit, trip

trick 1. *n* stunt, illusion, hoax, artifice, ploy, ruse, device, strategem, deception, subterfuge, wile, dodge, joke, trap, pretense

2. *vb* cheat, betray

trip 1. *n* journey, voyage, tour, excursion, expedition, cruise, passage, drive, travel, jaunt, outing, spin, pilgrimage, odyssey

2. *vb* stumble, slip, lurch, sprawl, fall

3. *vb* dance

trivial *adj* petty, trifling, unimportant, negligible, frivolous, paltry, piddling, insignificant, meager, small, minute, minor, mere, superficial

trouble 1. *n* difficulty, predicament, plight, problem, matter, quandary, fix, pinch, strait, pickle, jam, spot, ordeal, mischief, hardship, nuisance

2. *vb* inconvenience, distress, afflict, ail, harry, bother, disturb, worry

truth 1. *n* truthfulness, verity, authenticity, veracity, candor, sincerity, openness, accuracy, honesty, certainty ANTONYM: *lie*

2. *n* certainty

try 1. *vb* attempt, strive, struggle, essay, endeavor, venture, undertake, tackle, take on

2. *vb* test, sample, check, taste, experiment

3. *vb* prosecute, sue, indict, adjudicate, impeach, arraign, blame

4. *n* attempt, bid, endeavor, go, effort, trial, shot, stab, whirl

turn 1. *vb* spin, revolve, rotate, twirl, swirl, whirl, wheel, swivel, pivot, gyrate, wind, coil, hinge, flip, bend, swing, swerve

2. *n* curve, corner, round

type 1. *n* kind, sort, class, nature, manner, style, category, species, variety, race, breed, strain, genre, make

2. *n* print

ugly *adj* unsightly, repulsive, hideous, grotesque, loathsome, revolting, repellent, repugnant, horrid, grisly, plain ANTONYM: *pretty*

unaware *adj* ignorant, oblivious, obtuse, unmindful, unconscious, unconcerned, blind, deaf, heedless, naive

unbelievable *adj* incredible, unimaginable, implausible, improbable, indescribable, unlikely, impossible, doubtful

uncomfortable *adj* ill at ease, discomfited, cramped, painful, distressful, disagreeable, agonizing, anxious, nervous ANTONYM: *comfortable*

under 1. *prep* below, beneath, underneath ANTONYM: *above*

2. *prep* less than, lower than, inferior to, subject to, subordinate to

unfaithful *adj* false, traitorous, treacherous, disloyal, perfidious, false-hearted, fickle, dishonest ANTONYM: *faithful*

unfortunate *adj* unlucky, unhappy, hapless, disastrous, catastrophic, tragic, adverse, hapless, regrettable, lamentable, deplorable, sad, poor, pitiful

union 1. *n* unification, fusion, amalgamation, coupling, confluence, combination, marriage, merger, consolidation, link, wedding
2. *n* association, alliance, federation, league, partnership, guild, organization

unique *adj* unprecedented, incomparable, singular, peerless, unparalleled, unrivaled, unsurpassed, matchless, idiosyncratic, different, special, only

unnecessary *adj* needless, unessential, irrelevant, extraneous, superfluous, redundant, optional, gratuitous, pointless, extra, surplus, leftover, useless, excessive

unprepared *adj* unready, unsuspecting, inexperienced, napping, unwary

unreliable 1. *adj (used in reference to persons)* untrustworthy, irresponsible, fickle, undependable, unfaithful, dishonest ANTONYM: *reliable*
2. *adj (used in reference to ideas and inanimate objects or things)* deceptive, unsound, misleading, flimsy, wrong

upset 1. *vb* overturn, capsize, topple, upend, invert, tip
2. *vb n* defeat
3. *vb* worry, disturb, anger
4. *adj* angry
5. *n* shock

urban *adj* city, metropolitan, municipal, civic, cosmopolitan

urgent *adj* crucial, pressing, imperative, compelling, desperate, dire, acute, important

use 1. *vb* employ, utilize, wield, practice, exercise, exert, apply, expend, exploit, refer to, resort to, operate
2. *vb* consume, deplete, exhaust, expend, finish
3. *n* application, utilization, utility, usefulness, usage, purpose, operation, employment, consumption, expenditure, exercise, function, worth

useful *adj* helpful, practical, handy, beneficial, desirable, advantageous, profitable, pragmatic, utilitarian, versatile, efficient ANTONYM: *useless*

useless 1. *adj* futile, vain, fruitless, unavailing, hopeless, desperate, abortive, unsuccessful, ineffectual, unprofitable, unnecessary ANTONYM: *useful*

2. *adj* worthless, unusable, ineffective, counterproductive, broken

usual *adj* regular, customary, accustomed, habitual, ordinary, normal, set

vacation *n* holiday, recess, leave, furlough, sabbatical, respite, rest, R & R, break, leisure

valuable *adj* precious, dear, cherished, prized, beloved, inestimable, important, worthwhile, priceless, expensive, rare

variable *adj* changeable, unsettled, mutable, erratic, uncertain, uneven, inconsistent, arbitrary, fickle, unsteady

verify *vb* determine, prove, confirm, ascertain, ensure, assure, show, demonstrate, establish, authenticate, corroborate, substantiate, vindicate, defend, decide

vertical *adj* perpendicular, upright, erect, plumb, steep

very *adv* extremely, unusually, greatly, absolutely, immensely, terribly, awfully, rather, really, quite, most, too, much

victory *n* triumph, conquest, subjugation, mastery, overthrow, ascendancy, win ANTONYM: *defeat*

view 1. *n* sight, glimpse, scene, scenery, vision, panorama, outlook, spectacle, perspective, prospect, vista, look

2. *n* belief

3. *vb* look, study

4. *vb* believe

violent 1. *adj* savage, fierce, furious, fuming, enraged, berserk, angry, belligerent, mean, wild, destructive

2. *adj* strong, stormy

virtue 1. *n* integrity, morality, honor, trustworthiness, principle, decency, goodness, truth, honesty, kindness

2. *n* innocence, purity, modesty, chastity, virginity

3. *n* advantage, worth

visible *adj* observable, discernible, perceptible, perceivable, visual, optical, graphic, illustrative, obvious

visit 1. *vb* call on/upon, stay with, drop by/in, sojourn, frequent, travel

2. *n* call, stay, appointment, sojourn, visitation, get-together

voluntary *adj* intentional, deliberate, willful, willing, freely, spontaneous, optional

vote 1. *n* ballot, election, referendum, poll, polls, tally, choice

2. *vb* choose, decide

vulnerable *adj* defenseless, unarmed, unprotected, unguarded, susceptible, prone, disposed, weak

wage *n* salary, pay, allowance, fee, tip, compensation, income, earnings, profit, intake, stipend, revenue, return, pension

wait *vb* remain, linger, loiter, stay, tarry, await, abide, dally, delay, hesitate ANTONYM: *leave*

walk 1. *vb* amble, stroll, march, step, hike, stride, trudge, plod, lumber, file, trek, traipse, tramp, wander, strut, crawl

2. *n* gait

3. *n* path

want 1. *vb* wish, desire, crave, yearn, long, pine, hanker, itch, envy, hope, prefer

2. *vb* need

3. *n* lack, dearth, paucity, shortage, scarcity, deficiency, absence, hardship, poverty

warn *vb* forewarn, caution, alert, tip off, advise, admonish, exhort, counsel, scare, tell

waste 1. *vb* squander, fritter away, dissipate, misuse, misspend ANTONYM: *save*

2. *vb* decrease

3. *n* trash

4. *n* desert

5. *adj* sterile

wave 1. *n* billow, swell, surge, tidal wave, ripple, breaker, roller, whitecap, comber, surf

2. *vb* motion, gesture, signal, beckon, flag, salute

3. *vb* flutter, flap, ripple, sway, blow, swing

weak *adj* frail, feeble, infirm, invalid, helpless, powerless, unfit, impotent, puny, delicate, fragile, flimsy, rickety, breakable, thin, sick, vulnerable ANTONYM: *strong*

wealth *n* riches, affluence, means, opulence, luxury, prosperity, assets, fortune, treasure, hoard, money, property, abundance

weather 1. *n* climate, conditions, clime

2. *vb* age, season, wear, endure, harden

3. *vb* expose, overcome, bear

weight 1. *n* heaviness, heft, mass, substance, pressure, load, density, measure

2. *n* importance

welcome 1. *vb* greet, receive, salute, address, herald, hail, call, entertain, appreciate

2. *n* greeting, salutation, reception

3. *n* hospitality

well 1. *adv* properly, thoroughly, competently, satisfactorily, adequately, excellently, splendidly

2. *adv* favorably, kindly, approvingly, highly

3. *adj* healthy

4. *n* spring, reservoir, cistern, fountain, source

5. *n* shaft, bore, hole

wet 1. *adj* soaked, drenched, saturated, sodden, soggy, dripping, damp, liquid ANTONYM: *dry*

2. *adj* rainy, drizzly, stormy, inclement, misty, showery, snowy, slushy

3. *vb* moisten, soak, dampen, sprinkle, saturate, drench, douse, water, steep, immerse, rinse

white *adj* ivory, milky, snowy, silvery, snow-white, frosty, creamy, fair, pale ANTONYM: *black*

wild 1. *adj* untamed, fierce, ferocious, savage, raging, turbulent, fiery, violent, mean, rough, stormy

2. *adj* uncultivated, overgrown, rampant, overrun

3. *adj* disorderly, unruly, obstinate, undisciplined, stubborn

4. *n* country

will 1. *n* willpower, determination, resolution, volition, conviction, resolve, willfulness, ambition

2. *n* testament, bequest, inheritance

3. *vb* leave

win 1. *vb* triumph, prevail, succeed, overcome, defeat ANTONYM: *lose*

2. *vb* score, achieve, earn, get

3. *n* victory

wisdom *n* judgment, reason, understanding, appreciation, intelligence, intellect, comprehension, sagacity, perception, discernment, sense, common sense, knowledge, experience, depth

word 1. *n* term, expression, locution, utterance, vocable, verbalism, articulation, syllable

2. *n* talk

3. *n* promise

work 1. *n* labor, toil, effort, drudgery, exertion, industry, endeavor, pains, travail

2. *n* job, profession

3. *n* accomplishment, undertaking, composition, creation, opus, act, book, picture, poem

4. *vb* toil, labor, strive, struggle, slave, strain act, do

5. *vb* work out, solve

worry 1. *n* concern, care, anxiety, apprehension, burden, fear

2. *vb* upset, concern, trouble, fret, brood, stew, disturb, bother

worst *adj* meanest, lowest, bad, least ANTONYM: *best*

worth *n* value, benefit, merit, virtue, estimation, importance, price, use

wrap 1. *vb* gift wrap, cover, bind, envelop, shroud, clothe, swathe, sheathe, swaddle, bandage

2. *n* shawl, muffler, cloak, cape, mantle, stole, scarf

write 1. *vb* inscribe, jot, record, scribble, scrawl, transcribe, sign

2. *vb* compose, draft, indite, pen, author, publish, edit, compile, print

wrong 1. *adj* incorrect, false, mistaken, inaccurate, untrue, erroneous, invalid, bad, corrupt, amiss, awry, improper, illogical, immoral ANTONYM: *correct, right*

2. *n* crime

X ray 1. *n* radiation, ultraviolet ray, gamma ray

2. *n* radiograph, encephalogram, photograph

yell *vb* call, shout, scream, shriek, screech, bellow, thunder, rant, rave, harangue, boo, hiss, jeer, hoot, squall, cry

yes *interj* aye, okay, OK, affirmative, amen, certainly ANTONYM: *no*

young *adj* youthful, immature, juvenile, adolescent, boyish, girlish, underage, childish, new ANTONYM: *old*

zero *n* nothing, naught, nought, none, nil, love *(in tennis),* cipher

zone 1. *n* area, region, district, belt, band, quarter, place

2. *vb* divide

Index